# THE NATURAL FOODS
## *Sweet-Tooth Cookbook*

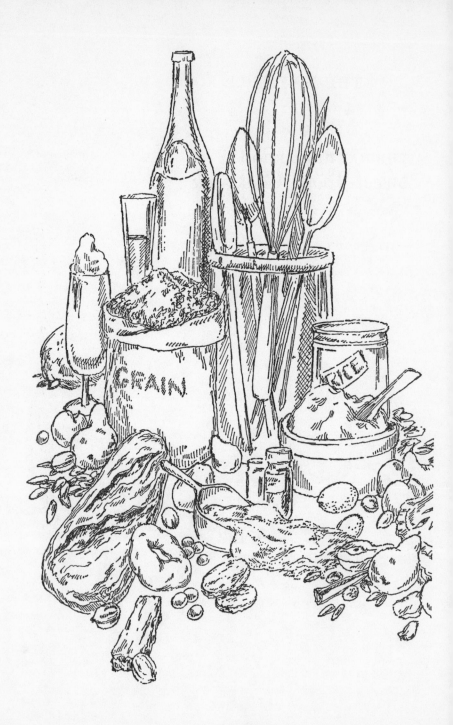

# THE NATURAL FOODS
# *Sweet-Tooth Cookbook*

BY EUNICE FARMILANT

DRAWINGS BY ED NUCKOLLS

DOUBLEDAY & COMPANY, INC.

GARDEN CITY, NEW YORK

1973

*Also by Eunice Farmilant:*

MACROBIOTIC COOKING

ISBN: 0-385-03568-3
Library of Congress Catalog Card Number 73–83588
Copyright © 1973 by Eunice Farmilant
All Rights Reserved
Printed in the United States of America
First Edition

*This book is dedicated with love to all Americans—fat, skinny, young, middle-aged, or in their second childhoods—just about anyone who enjoys good food and wants to maintain the best possible state of health at the same time. It is the hope of the author that you too will discover the joys of cooking with foods that offer the best way to this goal.*

# Acknowledgments

A very special thank you to all my friends in Boston, San Francisco, and Chicago, my brother Stephen, my sister Betsy, and my parents, who were often unknowing guinea pigs for most of the recipes developed for this book. Also to my dentist, Dr. Frank Garfin, for his supportive words and advice. The whole staff at the Food for Life store in Chicago and all the other people who contributed their ideas and warm encouragement.

# Contents

*Capitalized recipes may be located by consulting the Index.*

# Introduction

About five years ago my father and brother introduced my family to the concept of eating whole, natural foods. However, it took several months before my father's enthusiasm became so contagious that I, too, was bitten by the bug and followed his footsteps to the health food stores seeking out many new varieties of foods.

Struggling with a rigid diet and eating foods I didn't really enjoy had never appealed to me. As a teen-ager I had gone on many crash diets and had even experimented with being a vegetarian for almost a year, but I always regained the weight I lost in a matter of months. But this new approach to eating, which involved eliminating all kinds of refined foods (including sugar), not only made me feel better, but I also lost thirty pounds that I have not regained.

I had always loved to cook and experiment with new recipes, so it wasn't long before I discovered that many favorite dishes —especially desserts and snack foods—could be successfully created by using whole, natural foods in place of refined products.

I started out originally by using whole-wheat flour wherever white flour was called for in recipes, and replaced butter and margarine with vegetable oils. In place of cow's milk, I would use soy milk or soybean flour and water. But for sweetening certain desserts, finding a good substitute became a problem. Artificial sweetening agents were definitely out of the question because they are coal-tar derivatives and are not metabolized as food.

I discovered that fruit juices were great natural sweeteners, and besides, an eight-ounce portion of apple juice is only eighty calories, compared to 180 in an equal amount of milk. I would add protein-rich nuts and seeds as well as soybean flour to replace the nutrients found in milk.

As you can well imagine, my search for new ways of making desserts often led me out of the kitchen and into library reference books to research the nutritional value of foods. I also talked to many doctors and my own dentist, who hasn't used any sugar in his own house in years. Most of the doctors I met agreed that our diet, the typical American fare, that is, had become too rich; we were eating large amounts of empty foods that supplied lots of calories but not enough nutrients (like those gooey but deadly triple-layer frosted cakes that tempt us in magazines and bakery windows).

Milk is a wholesome food from a technical point of view, but many doctors have come to discover that it is not the best food for humans and not a perfect substitute for mother's milk. Besides being high in calories and fat content, it does contain valuable vitamins and minerals as well as protein. Contrary to its original intention pasteurization destroys much of the value contained in milk. Vitamins C, E, K, $B_1$ and riboflavin are altered along with enzymes. Pasteurized milk also lacks lactobacilli, which are destroyed by preservatives found in milk. Lactobacilli decompose sugar and produce lactic acid; they produce vitamins $B_1$, $B_2$, and $B_{12}$; they produce a growth factor that enables children to develop and are good for the prevention of food poisoning. However, raw milk does contain all the known vitamins, but it is extremely difficult to obtain today. But most of these nutrients can be obtained from other sources. Sesame seeds for instance, contain 1,600 milligrams of calcium in ¼ pound versus 590 milligrams in 2 cups of whole milk, and a quarter pound of carob flour contains 352 milligrams.

Preparing desserts with the aid of natural sweeteners is not a new concept in cooking. Refined sugar has been available on a large scale for only the past several hundred years, and there have been many times in modern man's history when he simply couldn't obtain it. During World War II, for instance, when there was an acute shortage of many foods, people throughout Europe had very little sugar or butter and were forced to use whole-wheat flour. Government documents from Great Britain and other European countries prove that the incidence of many diseases actually decreased during these times of hardship—lack of many of our so called "luxury foods" actually improved people's health!

Today there are many things we take for granted including the endless variety of foods available in our supermarkets. Often we overindulge in foods that satisfy our desire and need for sweets but don't satisfy our nutritional needs.

Well, you may ask yourself, what's wrong with using a little sugar now and then to make foods taste sweet? The problem today is that we are almost constantly surrounded by foods that already contain sugar. Statistics indicate that the average person's intake of sugar is rapidly approaching almost two hundred pounds a year.

We have become a nation of weight-watchers, yet we are notoriously attracted to sweets. Sugar consumption in America is among the highest per capita in the world. Dr. John Yudkin, a distinguished professor of nutrition at London University, in England, describes in detail many of the serious effects excessive sugar consumption has had on our health.* In addition to tooth decay, he relates many major diseases, including heart disease, to sugar consumption. He points out that the addition of sugar to all commercial and bottled baby foods, besides soft drinks and sweetened cereals and all the other treats children consume, has greatly increased the number of fat children.

Also, he states, "You may find it difficult to believe, but when you have really become used to taking very little sugar in your food and drinks, you will notice that all your foods have a wide range of interesting flavors that you had forgotten. Swamping everything with sugar tends to hide the flavors and blunts the sensitivity of your palate. You will especially notice how much you enjoy fruit—all the subtle difference between one sort of apple or pear or orange and another."

* Yudkin, Dr. John, *Sweet and Dangerous,* New York, Peter H. Wyden, Inc., 1972.

But natural ingredients have been used in this book not only for health reasons, but also for their superior taste and flavor. Natural fruit sugar can be just as concentrated as refined sugar, but it hasn't been subjected to chemicals, and, in addition, it contains valuable minerals. Also, the type of sugar found in whole foods is more complex than the refined sugar you buy in a store. Natural fruit and grain sugars are absorbed differently by the body, and additionally they contain nutrients that aid in digestion and assimilation. They also take more time to be digested, since they must first be broken down into simpler forms.

What about brown and raw sugar? The amounts of vitamins and minerals in both of these products is very small—just a smidgen more than in white sugar.

Ecologically, natural foods are the most logical ingredients to use. Refined flour and sugar have not only lost most of the original nutrients (refined sugar is almost completely devoid of any food value except calories), but the refining process itself is costly in terms of manpower and energy and more expensive in the long run because of all the waste that is produced.

Fresh fruits are cheaper when used in season. Therefore, the recipes given are designed to follow the availability of goods according to season. Frozen or canned foods are never used. Dried fruit that has been sun-dried rather than treated with sulfur dioxide is another handy natural sweetener and rich in nutrients as well.

Honey and maple syrup have been omitted intentionally for similar reasons. Tastewise, many foods contain so much natural sweetness that adding extra sweetness in the form of cane sugar, honey, or even maple syrup is unnecessary. Also, many leading nutritionists, such as Adelle Davis, warn that, although honey is a naturally sweet food, it contains only small traces of nutrients and appears to cause tooth decay as quickly as does refined sugar. And many honey users often go overboard by eating large amounts that put on extra weight (honey is far more concentrated and higher in calories than table sugar). Besides, honey is not a food created for man—but for bees! Our greed for honey is quickly producing a world-wide honey shortage.

DDT and other pesticides have drastically reduced the number of bees. Honey production has also been decreasing because many beekeepers are selling all the honey bees produce, rather than reserving some for the bees during the winter months. As a result, bees are fed sugar water, which weakens them, and their numbers continue to decrease. From just the ecological viewpoint, honey is not an ideal sweetening agent.

Maple syrup and forms of molasses are also refined products to some extent—ecologically maple syrup is a poor food because many gallons of sap must be concentrated through high heat to form crystallized sugar or syrup. Real maple syrup is a much better food than cane sugar, but it is very expensive and often hard to find.

If you are just getting accustomed to breaking the refined sugar habit, you may want to add a little honey or maple syrup to any of the recipes in this book during your withdrawal phase. However, I suggest that you first test the recipes without depending upon these concentrated sweetening agents and experience the honest sweetness of natural foods.

Starting from scratch with natural foods doesn't mean that you have to spend hours cooking. The recipes are suited to the modern kitchen and its many conveniences and to the homemaker who is often pressed for time. I have tried to use common ingredients that are easy to obtain and also economical.

Healthful desserts don't have to be dull! Many of the ideas for the recipes were culled from exotic Far Eastern dishes, traditional European favorites, and typical American cuisine—only some of the ingredients have been changed to protect as well as improve our health and diet.

In addition, the recipes are lower in calories than most dessert recipes, yet higher in nutritional value. They may be enjoyed by anyone including people on a restricted fat or low cholesterol diet, or by a diabetic who can't have any sugar; also young children who crave sweets and by teen-agers who need a high carbohydrate intake but worry about complexion and weight problems.

I firmly believe that good food should not only be nutritionally

satisfying but should captivate the senses and appeal to everyone. This approach to cooking can open an exciting field of ex-
ploration to the experienced cook as well as the novice anxious
to learn to make wholesome yet appetizing desserts.

# Part I

## An Organic Primer of Natural Foods and Other Tidbits

Cooking involves a bit of alchemy and common sense along with basic materials and utensils. Two cooks can start from scratch with the same materials and recipes, but the results may be entirely different. One essential facet of cooking depends upon attitude—just how you feel about the foods you're working with and whom you are cooking for can greatly affect the end result.

Because many of the foods used in this book may be new to people just discovering what natural cooking is all about, this section serves as a form of explanation and guideline.

Our food-buying habits are directly influenced by the amount of time, money, and energy we have for shopping. Sometimes it is difficult to travel to a health food store to obtain a certain ingredient or two, especially if the store is located on the other side of town. For this reason I have listed all the ingredients used in this book in the chapter *Stocking Your Organic Pantry.* However, it can be expensive to go out and buy all the ingredients at once, so I suggest that you start out gradually, by testing some recipes to see which foods appeal to you the most.

One alternative to being dependent upon health food stores is to investigate local food co-operatives. Almost every town and city has one or several going. Many of them operate through universities, churches, or natural food stores. Or, check for listings of such co-operatives in a local newspaper, or an alternative life style magazine such as *Mother Earth News.*

# Chapter 1. *Some Hints About Natural Sweeteners*

For many reasons, this book excludes concentrated and refined sweetening agents and provides alternative methods of preparing foods with natural sweeteners. Rather than honey, maple syrup, or brown sugar, barley malt extract is recommended, both because of its nutritional properties as well as its unrefined nature.

Almost all fruits and grains become sweeter the longer they are cooked. As the excess liquids are cooked out and the natural sugars broken down, the sweetness becomes more concentrated. Cooking is a form of alchemy—the art of changing foods and flavors through the use of time, pressure, and fire.

Organic apple juice or other fruit juices are convenient to use as quick sweeteners in cooking, and so are many kinds of dried fruit. Other liquids, such as grain coffees (those that are made from whole roasted grains and are commercially available in health food stores), and herbal teas can also be used to flavor desserts.

Salt also helps to bring out the natural sweetness of foods. However, too much salt can sometimes make a dessert taste slightly sour.

Pan roasting grains or flour in a dry cast-iron skillet before mixing with other ingredients gives them a richer, almost nutty taste. This step is recommended in many recipes.

# Chapter 2. *Stocking Your Organic Pantry*

Ideally, it is best to use the most natural unrefined foods available. They have the best taste and flavor and are certainly more healthful. The sources for these foods are places that specialize in them—natural food stores, health food stores, and specialty sections of supermarkets. If you can't find some of the foods you need, ask a local store to order them for you, or consult the shopping guide at the end of this book. These foods sometimes cost a little more money, item per item, than many commercial brand name products, but there are many advantages in terms of health that more than compensate for the price difference. However, creating your own desserts from scratch is usually much more economical than using prepared mixes, prepared frozen foods, and canned goods, and your own desserts certainly taste better!

DRIED FRUIT

Dried apples, apricots, cherries, currants, dates, figs, pears, peaches, prunes, and raisins can all be used interchangeably when dried fruit is called for in recipes. Store dried fruit in airtight glass jars. Refrigeration is necessary if you will be keeping the fruit for long periods of time, and especially important during the summer. It is important to get fruit that has been grown without chemical sprays and is sun-dried. Many supermarket varieties have been treated with sulfur dioxide, a chemical that speeds the drying process.

## FLOUR

Fresh flour should always be used for any kind of baking. The longer flour is stored, the more nutrients it loses. Whole grain flours have a short "shelf life"—that is, they do not stay fresh for long periods of time—because they contain oils that have a tendency to turn rancid. Flours that are kept too long usually taste bitter and should be discarded.

Stone-ground flours are best because of the lower temperatures the grain is subjected to during the milling process. Most of the big brand name flour companies use high-speed milling, a process that creates higher temperatures that alter the food value of the flour.

All purchased flour should be used as soon as possible. It is better to buy it in small quantities. Refrigerate grain flours in sealed containers. Ideally, the best way to obtain flour is to invest in an inexpensive grain mill. That way you can grind any flour or crack grain at home, and it will always be fresh. An electric blender can also be used for grinding flour. Whole grain that has not been milled will keep for months.

## FRESH FRUIT

Whenever possible, use fruit that is in season. It will be more in harmony with your environment and is much more ecological. Try to use fruit that comes from unsprayed orchards. If you are using nonorganic fruit, peel the skins. Fresh fruit is frequently waxed to extend its shelf life in addition to being coated with chemical sprays. Peeling is not necessary for fruit grown without sprays.

Because most tropical fruit is imported, and U.S. laws require it to be fumigated, it is omitted from this book. Therefore, bananas, pineapples, and other tropical fruits are not used.

LEAVENING AGENTS

Baking soda, baking powder, and yeast produce rapid reactions in pastry and bread dough, creating a breakdown in the chemical structure of food and a quick release of energy in the form of gas. Leavened foods stimulate the production of gastric acid during digestion, which shortens the time food remains in the stomach. Baking soda neutralizes stomach acids and can interfere with digestion so that the body is not able to absorb certain foods properly. Baking powder usually contains small amounts of baking soda. Many good cooks have learned to prepare desserts without these two leavening products. Unyeasted, naturally fermented bread assures a fermentation that transforms proteins into amino acids. This biological step creates a friendly environment favorable to the development of Phytase. Phytase effectively neutralizes phytic acid, which is always present in yeasted bread and detrimental to the absorption of many essential minerals by the body. Unleavened breads, cakes, cookies, and muffins are not quite as light as fast-yeasted batters, but they are just as delicious and far more chewy. Yeast is used in several recipes; when it is called for, try to use the dry yeast carried in the health and natural food stores. Naturally fermented grains and eggs can also be used to give a leavening effect.

NUTS AND SEEDS

As with commercially prepared dried fruit, many varieties of nuts and seeds are treated with chemicals. I can never understand the necessity of food manufacturers' habit of bleaching the shells of walnuts and almonds when they are only discarded and never consumed, but I suppose they think it makes them more attractive to the shopper. Shelled varieties are unfortunately treated in chemical baths that help to dissolve the outer shells and skins. I most heartily recommend sticking to health food varieties— they are of a superior quality and often less expensive than supermarket varieties.

NUT BUTTERS AND OILS

You can make sesame, almond, cashew, or peanut butter at home if you have a grain mill or electric blender. Roast the nuts before grinding and grind just once if using a grain mill. Salt can be added after grinding. When purchasing nut or seed butters look for those that are made from unbleached nuts or seeds.

Use pure, unrefined vegetable oils wherever oil is called for in the recipes. Natural food stores and many supermarkets now carry excellent grades of corn, safflower, sesame seed, sunflower seed, and soybean oil. Natural oils are free of preservatives and do not need refrigeration because they do not break down as quickly as refined oils, which have had many essential nutrients removed. Hydrogenated vegetable oils are not recommended because they are highly saturated fats. Natural, unrefined oils are rich in color and smell exactly like their sources—they are also higher in essential fatty acids and vitamins.

SALT

In all the recipes where salt is used, sea salt is recommended. Sea salt is different from rock salt or kosher salt, which come from old ocean deposits that dried on land. Sea salt is extracted from ocean water and is full of trace minerals. It is more expensive than plain table salt, but since only pinches of salt are used in cooking, the cost is negligible.

WHOLE GRAIN

Whole grain is much more alive than grain that has been milled. It can be stored for long periods of time in a cool, dry place provided it is kept in bags that allow for circulation of air.

Whole grain can be used in breads and batters if it is first cooked or soaked overnight. Cracked grain should be boiled or scalded; and flakes need a gentle roasting to freshen them before using with other ingredients.

Barley, buckwheat, corn, millet, rice, rye, and wheat can all be found in natural food stores.

MISCELLANEOUS

*aduki beans*—These are dark red Japanese beans. They are found in many Oriental food stores as well as health food stores. They are delicious in desserts and combine well with fruits.

*agar-agar*(or kanten)—A versatile gelatin derived from seaweed, agar-agar finds its way into many dessert preparations. It sets at room temperature, is clear and almost tasteless, full of minerals, but low in calories. It can be used in harmony with a variety of ingredients.

*barley malt extract*—This is a concentrated sweetening agent made from whole barley in a special process; it is not heavily processed or refined. It has a strong flavor and is used occasionally in this book. Be sure to purchase only pure barley malt extract. It is available in health food stores and stores that carry supplies for home brewing of wine and beer. It is very rich in minerals, proteins, and vitamins, unlike other concentrated sweetening agents, such as maple syrup or honey.

*carob*—Carob flour or powder is ground from the pods of the carob tree and has a flavor similar to that of chocolate. Known since biblical times as "St. John's bread," this valuable food is about 75 per cent carbohydrate and rich in natural sugars. It is very low in fat (unlike chocolate) and is a relatively good source of protein. Several tablespoons may be added to batters to replace some of the flour, to give a chocolate flavoring.

*chestnuts*—Dried chestnuts are carried in most Middle Eastern and Oriental markets as well as health food stores. They must be soaked for best results in cooking. Fresh chestnuts are available in late fall and winter. Chestnut flour is a heavy, sweet flour that can be used to sweeten cookie doughs and cake and bread batters as well as puddings.

*dandelion coffee*—This beverage is made from the roots of the dandelion plant and can be used in place of water or other liquid in many recipes. To prepare, use one heaping teaspoon of coffee for each cup of water and simmer for ten to fifteen minutes.

*grain coffee*—Commercially prepared grain coffee is sold in natural and health food stores. It tastes similar to regular coffee but is free of toxins and caffeine. Pero, made in Germany, is one brand that comes in an instant form and may be prepared like instant coffee.

*herbal tea*—When a recipe calls for liquid, herbal tea can be used in place of water or fruit juice. In the summer, spearmint, peppermint, and sassafras tea are fun to use in recipes containing fresh fruit. In the winter and fall, stronger tea, such as mu tea (a blend of sixteen herbs) or any other fragrant tea, adds a special spicy fragrance to cookies and breads.

*koji*—This is a form of fermented rice that has been treated with a special yeast culture. It is used in making amasake (fermented sweet rice) for sweetening desserts. It is carried in Oriental food stores.

*kuzu*—A thickening agent extracted from the roots of a mountain plant. It can be used in place of arrowroot flour starch. It is found in health and natural food stores.

*soy milk*—It can be used in place of water or other liquid in many recipes. It can be purchased or made at home. See the Index for directions for home preparation.

*starch*—Arrowroot flour starch is preferred as a thickening agent over cornstarch because of the former's purity and superior quality. It cooks very quickly and never leaves a chalky taste. Also, it has more nutritional value than cornstarch.

# Chapter 3. *A Few Words About Natural Condiments*

The best flavoring agents are those that accent, compliment, and blend harmoniously with foods. Pure, whole products are always recommended, not only for their superior flavor compared to powders or extracts, but also because of their freshness. Although most flavorings have little food value, their enhancement of foods that do have high nutritive value is a positive asset for the cook who is trying to create healthful dishes. Try to avoid commercially prepared spices; these are usually treated with chemicals during manufacturing.

*anise*—This is the dried fruit of an annual herb belonging to the parsley family. It adds a wonderful flavor to cake and cookie batters, and is also good in beverages.

*cinnamon*—This common spice comes from the inner bark of an evergreen tree. I find the sticks to be vastly superior to powdered cinnamon. They can be grated by hand in a mortar or ground in an electric blender. Or they can be used whole by infusing (simmering the spice in a saucepan with liquid for ten to twenty minutes).

*coriander*—This is the dried fruit of an annual herb belonging to the parsley family. It grows wild in Europe and Asia Minor and is cultivated in the United States. It has as much versatility as cinnamon and combines well with other flavorings.

*ginger*—Fresh gingerroot will keep for long periods of time if stored in a cool, dry cupboard. Health food stores carry excellent grades of ground ginger.

*lemon*—Both the rind and juice of the lemon can be used for flavoring. Lemon extracts are handy to use; however, be sure to purchase pure extract and not imitation flavorings.

*nutmeg*—Because nutmeg can be intoxicating and even addictive in excessive quantities, use it sparingly and only occasionally. However, it does provide a distinctive flavor to certain dishes, and many cooks relish this condiment. As with all herbs and spices, it's a matter of personal taste.

*orange*—Orange juice and rind add a sharp accent to many desserts that need extra pizazz. Personally, I like to dry the skin, grate it, and store it in glass jars. Pure orange extract can also be used for flavoring.

*poppy seeds*—The mild flavor of poppy seeds makes them a welcome addition in many desserts and pastries. I find that rinsing the seeds in cold water and toasting them lightly before adding to other ingredients improve their flavor.

*sesame seeds*—Although these seeds are also a valuable food, they do lend a pleasant touch to many dishes. Try to obtain the natural brown sesame seeds from natural food stores (these may be purchased by the pound). Avoid the white, hulled varieties, which are often chemically bleached. Black sesame seeds are also available in some areas. Always rinse the seeds in cold water before using.

*tangerine*—It may be used for flavoring in the same way as oranges.

*vanilla beans*—Vanilla beans are used almost exclusively throughout this book instead of flavorings or extracts. Once you acquire the habit of using the whole bean, you'll discover the rewards are worth the extra trouble. If you prefer to use extracts, add them near the end of cooking. The beans may be used several times until their strength is diminished.

# Chapter 4. *Kitchen Ecology*

All the fancy pots and pans in the world don't necessarily make a good cook. You probably have all the essential items already—mixing bowls, Pyrex glass containers that can serve both as casseroles and mixing bowls, measuring spoons, etc. For making breads, ceramic bowls or wooden bowls are favored, but stainless steel or hard plastic are practical and easy to keep clean.

For stirring and mixing, wooden spoons are recommended because they don't scratch the surface of bowls or pans and will not bruise ripe fruit in dishes that require a light touch. They are also aesthetically pleasing. An electric mixer or blender is a convenience but not essential for every recipe. For most preparations a wire whisk or hand-operated egg beater can be substituted for a blender. A Foley food mill or vegetable grinder is helpful in making purées.

For crushing nuts and seeds a mortar and pestle or a Japanese suribachi, or a coffee grinder can be used, but a heavy rolling pin will also do the job.

A couple of saucepans, a pressure cooker or large pot with a tight-fitting lid and a cast-iron skillet are fairly essential items. Cookie sheets, bread and cake pans are also important items, but other kitchen utensils can be used in place of them with a little ingenuity. A glass jar can be substituted for a rolling pin.

Wooden boards are best for kneading and rolling out dough, but any clean surface covered with flour would be a good substitute.

# Chapter 5. A Glossary of Grains

Organically grown grains taste sweeter and make better breads, muffins, cookies, and cakes when the flour is as fresh as possible. An inexpensive hand mill is a good investment if you plan on making your own breads and cookies frequently. When whole grain is ground into flour, some of the value of the grain is destroyed by the milling process. For this reason it is preferable to use some whole cooked grain in batters—it also makes an end product that is lighter and easier to digest. For these reasons, wherever possible, the recipes incorporate some whole cooked grains in the listing of ingredients.

Because natural flour begins to turn rancid through oxidation (oxidation means contact with air; this starts to occur just sixteen hours after the grain has been milled), it is recommended that all flours be gently pan-roasted before using in recipes, unless, of course, you are using flour that was just ground. Flours purchased from natural food stores should be used as soon as possible to prevent spoilage, and refrigeration is essential to retain the best qualities of the flour.

Whole grain and grain flours are now being sold in natural food stores all over the country. Some supermarkets are starting to stock natural foods, and most stores will be happy to stock whole grain flours if customers ask for them. Be sure to buy flour that has not been enriched or treated for a long shelf life. If you can't find an immediate source for flour, consult the Guide to Natural and Health Food Stores in Part III.

*barley*—Barley is a small-kerneled cereal grain characterized by a fine brownish line running down the center which almost separates the grain into two tiny chambers. Its digestibility has long been recognized by physicians, who recommend it as a baby food. Barley cultivation dates back to prehistoric times, and it originated somewhere in Syria and Northern Egypt.

Cooked alone as a grain, it is similar to rice. Barley flour is sweet and light and has a wonderful texture. Its unique taste and pearly white color can be used most advantageously in making cookies or puddings.

*bran*—Bran comes from the outer layers of grain. It is coarse in texture but very light and rich in minerals. Light roasting improves flavor and eliminates any bitter taste. Wheat bran is usually easy to obtain in most natural food outlets. Rice bran is carried in some natural food stores and also in Japanese markets. Rice bran has similar qualities to wheat but is somewhat finer and heavier.

*buckwheat*—Buckwheat is a hearty member of the grass family, and although it is not a true cereal, botanically, it is closer to grains and is used as a flour. Roasted groats are easily ground into flour in a hand mill or electric blender. The heavy flour is sweet and excellent in breads, cakes, and cookie dough. Unroasted groats are greenish in color and have a slightly bitter taste; they should always be lightly roasted before grinding into flour.

*corn*—Cultivation of corn during the past few thousand years has created a number of different varieties. Corn grown for flour is large kerneled and commonly known as field corn. When buying whole corn for making your own flour at home, you will find two varieties available. White corn is somewhat sweeter than yellow corn. If you are purchasing corn meal or corn flour, try to obtain a brand that has not been enriched or degerminated. Corn meal is coarser than corn flour and is usually scalded or cooked before being used with other ingredients in breads or muffins.

*couscous*—This is a wheat product imported from the Near

East. It is light yellow but after cooking turns white and becomes very fluffy. It can be used as a cooked grain in breads, muffins, and cakes. It is carried in many European grocery stores as well as gourmet food sections in supermarkets, health and natural food stores.

*oats*—Although most of us are familiar with oat flakes, or rolled oats, few people have seen whole oat groats. Oat groats are soft and easily ground into a light flour that can be used in making puddings, breads, and cookies. Whole oat groats can be cooked as rice and used wherever cooked grain is called for in a recipe.

*millet*—Although a staple food of Asia and Europe for thousands of years, millet is used very little in this country. It is a very tiny grain, spherical in shape. It is easily ground into a fine flour that has a pleasant texture suitable for cakes and breads. Whole cooked millet is also used in bread batters and puddings. As with buckwheat, pan-roasted millet tastes better, otherwise it may develop a bitter taste.

*brown rice*—Whole brown rice is almost nutty in taste and an important ingredient in breads, cookies, and cakes. It can be ground into flour, puréed, or left whole.

Sweet brown rice is also used in many recipes. Because it is higher in gluten content and somewhat heavier and sweeter, it lends itself best to puddings or sweet breads.

*wheat*—There are many different kinds of wheat, each with distinguishing characteristics. Hard red wheats grown in Canada and the great plains of the United States are small, plump grains with excellent milling and baking qualities. These varieties are best for making breads and are high in gluten. They are usually grown in the spring. Hard red winter wheats are similar in appearance but slightly longer and thinner and have a lower gluten content.

Soft red wheats are weaker, and soft white wheats are the weakest. The white wheats are used in making whole-wheat pastry flour because the bran can be finely ground.

Different grades of wheat yield different results. Durum wheat, for example, is a hard wheat suitable for making macaroni noodles but a poor choice for baking light pastries. Learning the

different properties of wheat flours is very important—you may
have to alter recipes to allow for flour that has a higher moisture
content. If your flour is very dry, it will absorb more water and
you will probably have to add more liquid or perhaps oil.

# Part II
## Putting It
## All
## Together

Now that you have had some background information on what exactly is meant by natural foods, and the terminology used throughout this cookbook, it's time to put on an apron, take out some staples, and dive into the pots.

# Chapter 6. *Breads and Muffins*

Sweet breads served with a spread of nut or fruit butter make simple desserts or pleasing snacks. Bread batters are always fun to experiment with—the best breads are usually those that contain leftovers—it's a good way to use up the extra breakfast cereal, or a fruit dessert, or some extra nuts or seeds you happen to have on hand. For extra protein, soy flour is included in the ingredients in most of these recipes. Whole cooked grain is used whenever feasible to give lightness and added texture.

If you are fond of wheat germ, you can add a little in place of some of the flour. Or add rice or wheat bran to lend a nutty taste to the batter.

Fermented grain can be added to give a slight leavening effect. For breads that turn out best, a slow, steady oven is essential. If your oven has a tendency to heat unevenly, cover the pan with a piece of tin foil during the first half hour or forty-five minutes of baking time (so the bread will steam), then remove the cover during the remaining baking time for a firm but soft crust.

## Spicy Bean Bread
### (*Makes about 8 servings*)

Beans add a new dimension to making bread. This bread is sweet and dense but not terribly heavy. It is especially delicious with Apple Butter.

2 cups cooked black beans or soybeans
1½ cups grain coffee, mu tea, or water
1½ cups buckwheat flour
1¼ cups whole-wheat flour
¼ cup soybean flour
1 teaspoon sea salt
½ teaspoon each cinnamon, coriander, cloves
2 tablespoons corn germ oil
2 tablespoons sesame seeds

Preheat oven to 375° F.

Purée beans in a blender with grain coffee. Add remaining ingredients and continue to knead dough for about 5 minutes, until it becomes slightly elastic. Oil a large bread pan (9×5×3 inches) and, wetting your hands, shape the dough into a loaf and set in pan.

Cover the pan tightly with tin foil and bake for 1 hour. Remove foil and bake for another 20 minutes. Let cool for 1 hour before cutting. Serve with fruit butter or Nut Butter.

VARIATIONS: Add 3 tablespoons carob powder to batter for a chocolate flavor. For a sweeter bread, add ½ cup Amasake Syrup.

## *Spiral Cinnamon-Raisin Bread*
(*Makes about 9 servings*)

This recipe was inspired by the Bread Shop (a natural foods bakery) in Chicago. The spiral design appears when you cut the bread into serving pieces.

1 cup brown rice flour
1 cup white or yellow corn flour
4 cups liquid (grain coffee, mu tea, or apple juice)
1 cup raisins or currants
½ teaspoon sea salt
1½ cups whole-wheat pastry flour
¼ cup soybean flour
½ cup chopped nuts
1 tablespoon cinnamon
4 tablespoons Nut Butter (or natural peanut butter)
2 tablespoons fruit juice
Grated lemon or orange rind, optional

Pan-roast the rice and corn flours in a dry cast-iron pan until lightly toasted. Pour into a large mixing bowl and set aside.

Bring the 4 cups liquid to a boil with the raisins. Cover and simmer for 5 minutes. Holding a strainer over the mixing bowl, pour the hot liquid over the flours and reserve the raisins. Mix flours thoroughly with a wooden spoon until all the liquid is absorbed. Then add the salt, pastry flour, and soybean flour and mix again.

In a separate bowl, mix together the raisins, nuts, cinnamon, nut butter, juice, and rind. Spread the dough out on a well-floured bread board and flatten to about a 1-inch thickness. Coat the entire surface of the dough with the raisin mixture filling and roll up, like a jelly roll.

Transfer bread to a well-oiled pan and make a few slashes across the top with a sharp knife.

Cover bread with a damp cloth and place in a warm spot for a couple of hours. Preheat oven to 350° F. Bake for 40 minutes with a covering of tin foil. Remove foil and bake for another 30–40 minutes, or until lightly browned. Let cool for at least 30 minutes before cutting.

VARIATIONS: For cinnamon apricot bread, use orange juice in place of part of the liquid and replace raisins with 1 cup chopped dried apricots. Or you can try using chopped dried pears, figs, or peaches.


## Corn Spoon Bread
### *(Makes about 8 servings)*

This light and fragrant semisweet bread holds together well and will keep moist for several days if wrapped in waxed paper and stored in the refrigerator.

3 cups whole corn meal (not degerminated or enriched)
4 cups boiling apple juice
½ cup whole-wheat pastry flour
2 cups cooked brown rice (or bulgur, cracked wheat, or millet)
¼ cup corn or sesame oil
2 tablespoons sesame seeds, toasted
1 teaspoon sea salt
1 egg, optional
1 teaspoon cinnamon
¼ teaspoon coriander or nutmeg, optional

Preheat oven to 400° F.
Pan-roast the corn meal in a heavy skillet for 10 minutes, stirring constantly to prevent burning. Pour meal into a large bowl and scald with the apple juice. Pour the apple juice slowly and mix the batter thoroughly to prevent lumping. Let mixture sit for 10 minutes.
Add remaining ingredients, one at a time, beating well after each addition. Spoon batter into a well-oiled shallow 2-quart

casserole. Bake at 400° for the first 15 minutes, then reduce heat to 350° for another 40 minutes.

VARIATIONS: Chopped nuts, sunflower seeds, or chopped dried fruit can be added if desired. Soybean flour or chestnut flour can be substituted for part of the whole-wheat pastry flour.

## Date Nut Bread
### (*Makes about 12 servings*)

Bread dates are a drier variety of dates and lend themselves very well to dessert preparations.

1 cup bread dates, pitted
⅓ cup soybean flour
½ cup buckwheat or rye flour
1½ cups whole-wheat pastry flour
½ teaspoon sea salt
1 teaspoon cinnamon
½ teaspoon cloves
½ teaspoon nutmeg or coriander
1 cup cooked grain (any cereal)
1 cup chopped nuts
1½ cups liquid (fruit juice, grain coffee, or mu tea)
3 tablespoons sesame oil

If you have the time, refrigerate the dates for several hours in advance; this makes them harder so they are easier to pit.

Combine the dry ingredients. Add the liquids gradually. The batter should be rather wet and well mixed. Pour into a well-oiled casserole (about 10×15×2½ inches), cover with a damp cloth, and set in a warm spot for a couple of hours; or leave in the refrigerator for 12–24 hours.

Preheat oven to 350° F.

Bake for about 1½ hours. The top should be dark and firm to the touch. Store the bread in the refrigerator. It will stay fresh for several days or may be frozen for about a month.

## Gingerbread
(*Makes about 9 servings*)

Here's a recipe for gingerbread that's dark, moist, and spicy and nutritious enough to serve for breakfast. Fresh carrots and oat flakes are the magical ingredients that help to retain a chewy texture and unique flavor.

2 cups oat flakes
1½ pounds fresh carrots
A 2-inch piece of gingerroot
¾ cup chestnut flour (if none is available, use ½ cup soy flour)
½ cup buckwheat or rye flour
½ cup whole-wheat pastry flour
½ teaspoon sea salt
1 teaspoon cinnamon
¼ teaspoon nutmeg
1 tablespoon dry Pero (a grain coffee substitute)
1 tablespoon poppy seeds, optional
1 egg, optional
2 cups apple juice
¼ cup corn oil

Preheat oven to 375° F.

Dry-roast the oat flakes in a cast-iron skillet for about 10 minutes, or until golden in color. Stir constantly to prevent burning. Pour flakes into a large bowl and set aside.

Grate carrots either by hand or in a blender, being careful not to liquify them. If you prefer, use cooked and mashed carrots in place of raw carrots. To prepare the gingerroot, peel off the skin and finely grate the root. Squeeze out the juice and discard the stringy pulp.

Combine all ingredients and mix batter thoroughly. Pour into a shallow 9×15 inch baking dish that has been well oiled and bake for 1 hour and 15 minutes.

Serve either warm or cold. This bread is especially good when served with applesauce and garnished with slivered almonds or crushed walnuts.

## Holiday Fruit Nut Bread
(*Makes about 24 servings*)

Not quite as rich as fruitcake, this holiday treat makes a perfect buffet food at parties. It combines well with just about any fruit spread or nut or seed butter.

*Bread Batter:* (Prepare at least 8 hours in advance)
1 cup corn meal
4½ cups liquid (this can be grain coffee or strong herbal tea)
3 cups oat flakes
1 cup cooked grain (any cereal)
2 teaspoons sea salt
2 teaspoons spices (cinnamon, cloves, etc.)
2½ cups whole-wheat flour
*Remaining Batter:*
1 cup fruit juice
½ pound chopped dried fruit (or currants)
1 lemon
4 tart red apples
½ cup vegetable oil
1 pound coarsely chopped nuts
½ cup soybean or chestnut flour

To prepare the bread batter, first pan-roast the corn meal in a dry cast-iron skillet until it smells fragrant and is darkened slightly. Bring liquid to a boil. Pour the corn meal into a large bowl and scald with liquid. Set aside to cool.

Toast the oat flakes in a skillet until they are golden in color. Add to the scalded corn meal and mix well. Add grain, salt, and spices. Let sit for 10 minutes.

Beat in the whole-wheat flour and knead mixture for 10 minutes. Cover bowl with wet terry cloth and let sit undisturbed for at least 8 hours or overnight.

Preheat oven to 325° F.

Bring fruit juice to a boil, add dried fruit and simmer for 1 minute. Turn off flame and cover pan. This softens the fruit so it will remain moist during baking.

Using a fine grater, grate the entire lemon. Grate the apples coarsely. If you are using apples grown without sprays, peeling is not necessary; otherwise it is best to peel them.

Add dried fruit, lemon, and apples to bread batter, mixing thoroughly after each addition. Mix in remaining ingredients.

Oil 2 medium-size bread pans and fill to the top with batter. Bake for about 2½ hours, or when a wooden skewer inserted in the center comes out clean.

To serve, bread should be allowed to cool for at least 1 hour before cutting. It is similar to fruit nut cake in taste and appearance. It is especially delicious served with Apple or Sesame Butter.

It keeps without refrigeration for several days. If refrigerated, wrap tightly to retain moisture. Properly stored, it will stay fresh for up to a week.


## Lemon Sponge Millet Bread
(*Makes about 8 servings*)

This bread resembles spongecake in texture and appearance. It cuts beautifully. For extra sweetness, try adding ½ cup chopped bread dates or figs to the batter.

1 cup whole millet
3 cups apple juice
1 cup cooked cereal (brown rice, couscous, or oatmeal)
1½ cups whole-wheat pastry flour
2 tablespoons soybean or chestnut flour
1 teaspoon sea salt
½ cup coarsely chopped nuts
2 tablespoons oil
1 lemon
¼ teaspoon nutmeg, optional

Rinse the millet in cold water and drain through a fine strainer. Heat a cast-iron skillet and pour in the millet. Stirring constantly, roast the millet for about 10 minutes, until it is completely dry and lightly toasted. Add apple juice and bring to a boil; cover and simmer for 30 minutes.

Preheat the oven to 350° F.

Spoon cooked millet into a large mixing bowl and mash with a fork until the grains are separated. Mash in the cooked cereal, the flours, salt, nuts, and oil. Grate the lemon over a fine grater and add the rind and juice to the batter. Mix thoroughly and pour batter into a well-oiled bread or cake pan. Sprinkle top with nutmeg. Bake at 350° for 30 minutes, then reduce temperature to 325° and bake for another 50–60 minutes.

## *Oat Spoon Bread*
(*Makes about 8 servings*)

This is a simple, light dessert that forms a rich golden crust with a creamy pudding filling inside.

3 cups oat flakes
5 cups water
2½ cups cubed fall squash (butternut, buttercup, banana, or acorn)
½ teaspoon sea salt
3 apples, grated
3 tablespoons Sesame Butter or Almond Butter
½ cup whole-wheat pastry flour
2 tablespoons soybean or chestnut flour

Preheat oven to 350° F.

Place oats, water, squash, and salt in a large saucepan and bring to a boil. Cover and reduce flame. Simmer for 15 minutes.

Purée cooked oats and squash in a food mill or blender. Beat in remaining ingredients and pour into an oiled 2-quart casserole or large shallow cake pan. Bake for 1½ hours.

For variety, ½ cup chopped nuts can be used in place of nut butter. A dash of coriander, cinnamon, or nutmeg can be added if desired.

## Bran Muffins
(*Makes 1 dozen large or 18 medium muffins*)

2 cups wheat or rice bran
1 cup whole-wheat pastry flour
2 tablespoons soybean flour
1 teaspoon cinnamon
½ teaspoon sea salt
2 tablespoons roasted sesame seeds
2 tablespoons oil
1 cup apple juice
½ cup currants or chopped dried fruit
2 cups cooked cereal (any grain)

Preheat oven to 350° F. and insert muffin tins.

In a dry cast-iron skillet, pan-roast the bran, stirring constantly until the bran darkens and gives off a nutty fragrance. This helps to sweeten the flavor of the bran. Mix bran with flours, spice, salt, sesame seeds, and oil until mixture is fine and crumbly.

Bring apple juice to a boil in a saucepan and add fruit. Simmer for a few minutes. Pour liquid immediately over the bran mixture. Mix batter lightly and let stand for a few minutes. Then mix in cooked cereal and knead thoroughly for 5 minutes.

Remove muffin tins from oven and brush wells with oil. Fill muffin tins to the top and bake for 50–60 minutes.

VARIATIONS: These muffins are very sweet and chewy, but if you prefer lighter muffins, add an egg to the batter. Chopped nuts or sunflower seeds can be used in place of the sesame seeds.

## Corn Muffins
*(Makes 1 dozen large muffins)*

1½ cups corn meal
2 cups boiling water or apple juice
1 cup cooked cereal (rice, couscous, etc.)
2 tablespoons soybean or chestnut flour
2 tablespoons arrowroot flour starch
2 tablespoons sesame seeds
½ teaspoon sea salt
2 tablespoons corn or sunflower seed oil
1 egg, optional
1 cup fresh crushed fruit (blueberries or peaches)
1 teaspoon grated lemon rind

Preheat oven to 350° F. and insert muffin tins.

Pan-roast the corn meal in a dry skillet until golden in color. Pour into a mixing bowl and scald with water or apple juice. Stir rapidly to prevent lumping.

Beat in remaining ingredients. Remove muffin tins from oven and brush wells with oil. Spoon mixture to the top of each well. Bake for 45 minutes.

VARIATIONS: Puréed chestnuts or cooked and puréed dried fruit or chopped dates can be used in place of fresh fruit. Orange juice can be used in place of water for a surprising sunny taste.

## Oat Muffins
### (*Makes 18 large muffins*)

These very light muffins are made with relatively little flour because of the way the oat flakes are scalded before being mixed with the other ingredients.

3 cups oat flakes
2 cups fruit juice
½ cup currants or chopped dried fruit
1 cup whole-wheat pastry flour
½ teaspoon sea salt
½ teaspoon cinnamon
3 tablespoons vegetable oil
1 egg, optional

Preheat oven to 375° F. and insert muffin tins.

Pan-roast the oat flakes in a dry cast-iron skillet until golden in color; while the oats are being toasted, bring fruit juice and currants to a boil in a saucepan.

Pour the oat flakes into a bowl and, holding a strainer over the bowl, scald flakes with the juice, reserving the fruit. Let flakes sit for about 5 minutes to absorb liquid.

Beat in remaining ingredients. Remove muffin tins and brush wells with oil. Spoon batter almost to the top of each well. Bake for 15 minutes at 375°, then reduce temperature to 350° and bake for another 30 minutes.

VARIATIONS: Wheat flakes can be used in place of the oat flakes for chewy muffins. Also, ⅓ cup chopped nuts or sunflower seeds is a welcome addition.

# Chapter 7. Quick Batter Desserts

## Dessert Pancakes, Crêpes, and Fritters

Quick batter desserts are fun foods because they are so easy to mix up and take so little time to prepare and cook. The best crêpes are those that are whipped up spontaneously—these basic recipes are intended to serve as a guide for your imagination. Crushed nuts, mild spices, crushed fresh fruit, or chopped dried fruit can be added directly to the batter.

Crêpes are lighter than pancakes, and the thin batter contains less flour. They take less than a minute to cook. Always begin by heating the skillet before adding oil.

Fritters can be a mixture of flour, eggs, and fruit. The batter is thick and should hold together when dropped by a spoon into hot oil. Fritters need to be served while still hot from the stove, but crêpes and pancakes can be cooled and stored in the refrigerator and used up to several days later.

## *Apple Corn Fritters*
### (*Makes about 18 2-inch fritters*)

Crispy fruit fritters aren't especially elegant, but they are appealing because of their down-home flavor.

1 cup corn flour
2 cups boiling water or fruit juice
1 cup cooked grain (any cereal)
2 large apples, grated
¼ cup arrowroot flour starch
2 tablespoons soybean or chestnut flour
1 teaspoon sea salt
1 teaspoon cinnamon
1 quart safflower oil (for deep frying)

Scald the corn flour with the hot liquid. Stir quickly to avoid lumps and let cool. Add remaining ingredients except for oil and mix well.

Heat oil in a deep skillet, wok, or electric frying pan. Oil should be at least 2 inches deep at the center of pan. As soon as the oil is hot enough (about 350° F.), drop batter from a tablespoon into the pan. Fritters will first sink to the bottom of the pan and then rise to the top. Turn over once when they float to the top of the oil. With a slotted spoon remove when sides are lightly browned, and drain on paper towels.

To keep fritters hot, place on a cookie sheet and set in a moderately warm (325°) oven.

Serve fritters plain, with fruit butter, Soy Cream Sauce, or Vanilla Sauce.

## Baked Donuts
*(Makes 1 dozen 2-inch donuts)*

Here is a simple recipe for making donuts that have very little oil, because they are first boiled (like bagels) and then baked.

½ cup sweet brown rice flour
½ cup millet flour
½ cup whole-wheat pastry flour
2 tablespoons soybean flour
½ teaspoon cinnamon
1 cup apple juice
2 teaspoons sesame oil
2 teaspoons sea salt
6 cups boiling water

Preheat oven to 375° F.

Mix dry ingredients except salt in a bowl. Add juice and oil and knead thoroughly. Roll into spheres about the size of Ping-Pong balls and flatten slightly. Poke your finger in the center of each ball to make a hole.

Add salt to the boiling water and drop in donuts. Cook only a few at a time. When donuts float to the top and have almost doubled in size, remove with a slotted spoon. Brush with oil and place on an oiled cookie sheet. Bake for 15–20 minutes, or until the donuts are lightly browned and crispy. Serve warm.

VARIATIONS: Glaze with Apple Butter, Sesame Glaze, or Fresh Fruit Glaze.

## Blintzes
*(Makes about 15)*

1 cup unbleached white flour or whole-wheat pastry flour
1 cup water
2 beaten eggs
½ teaspoon sea salt
Dash of nutmeg or cinnamon
¼ cup sesame oil (for frying)

Beat all ingredients in a mixing bowl with a wire whisk. Transfer to a container with a spout for easy pouring. Or, if you prefer, a soup ladle can be used for measuring out the right amount of batter.

Heat a small cast-iron skillet. Test temperature with a drop of water—if it sizzles immediately, the pan is hot enough to begin. Brush pan with a small amount of oil. Pour a small amount of batter into pan and tip quickly to spread batter.

Blintzes take about 30 seconds to cook. Lift the edge of the pancake with a spatula to loosen it from the pan and then invert pan over a damp linen towel. Repeat cooking process until all batter is used up. Cover blintzes until ready to use.

Put a spoonful of your favorite filling (it can be applesauce, puréed fruit, etc.) in the center of each blintz and fold over the sides. The blintzes can now be sautéed in the skillet with more oil or baked in an oiled casserole until lightly browned.

## Buckwheat Crêpes
### (*Makes about 12*)

High-protein buckwheat combined with eggs makes a super crêpe that is loaded with nutrients as well as taste.

¾ cup buckwheat flour
¼ cup unbleached flour or whole-wheat pastry flour
1 tablespoon soybean flour or chestnut flour
1 cup water
2 eggs, beaten
½ teaspoon sea salt
½ teaspoon cinnamon
Sesame oil (for frying)

Combine all ingredients in a mixing bowl and lightly beat. Heat skillet and, when pan is hot, brush with oil.

Pour in a small amount of batter and quickly tilt pan to spread batter. Cook until the edges are set and air bubbles form over the surface. Turn pancakes over and fry until crisp. Remove with a spatula and place on a hot plate.

Batter will have a tendency to separate because buckwheat is a very heavy flour, so stir batter each time before pouring. These pancakes also take a little longer to cook, and it is important to make them as thin as possible.

Serve with Tangy Applesauce, Dried Fruit Purée, Fresh Fruit Glaze, or the quick filling suggested here:

Mix together 3 tablespoons of each: apple butter, almond butter, raisins, chopped nuts, and fruit juice. Add ½ teaspoon cinnamon or grated orange rind.

## Buckwheat Fritters
(*Makes about 30 bite-size fritters*)

These crunchy nuggets make a unique winter or cold weather dessert treat. They are a cross between a fried cookie and donut.

3 cups cooked buckwheat*
3 tablespoons arrowroot flour starch
¼ cup chestnut or soybean flour
1 teaspoon each: cinnamon, sea salt, coriander, or anise
2 tablespoons sesame seeds or crushed nuts
1 egg
1 cup grated apples or crushed fresh fruit
1 quart oil for frying

Mix all ingredients well. Heat oil in a deep skillet, wok, or electric frying pan. Drop batter by a spoonful at a time into the hot oil and deep-fry until browned on all sides. Remove with a slotted spoon or oil strainer and place on paper towels to drain. Serve hot with Tangy Applesauce, Soy Cream Sauce, or Vanilla Sauce.

* To prepare buckwheat: Bring 2½ cups water to a boil. Add 1 cup roasted buckwheat groats. Cover and simmer for 10–15 minutes. Rye or whole-wheat flakes may be used in place of buckwheat groats. Prepare in the same way as for buckwheat groats.

## Dessert Pancakes
(*Makes 12 9-inch crêpes*)

1 cup whole-wheat pastry flour
½ cup brown rice, barley, or oat flour
2 tablespoons chestnut or soybean flour
½ teaspoon sea salt
½ teaspoon cinnamon
1 teaspoon grated lemon or orange rind
1 cup water

½ cup fruit juice
1–2 eggs
2 tablespoons sesame or safflower oil

Combine all ingredients. Stir batter lightly in a mixing bowl. Heat a medium-size skillet and test with a drop of water. If it sizzles immediately, brush pan with oil.

Using a soup ladle or measuring cup, pour ¼ cup batter into skillet. Turn cakes over when bubbles form and the edges are set. Stir batter occasionally before pouring. Stack pancakes on a plate and keep in a warm oven until ready to serve. Pancakes may also be chilled and reheated.

Serve with Apple Butter, puréed fruit, or applesauce.

VARIATIONS: Add ½ cup crushed fresh fruit such as blueberries or peaches to batter. Almond or Sesame Butter can be used in place of oil in batter.

## French-Fried Apple Rings
*(Makes 4–6 servings)*

A new disguise for an old friend. This dessert is always a hit with apple lovers and will quickly win over new devotees.

4 large apples
½ teaspoon sea salt
Soybean flour
*Batter:*
⅔ cup liquid (mu tea, fruit juice, or water)
½ cup whole-wheat pastry flour
1 heaping tablespoon arrowroot flour starch or
   1 egg
½ teaspoon cinnamon
Oil for deep frying

Wash the apples and slice crosswise into rings ⅕ inch thick. Place rings on a platter and sprinkle with sea salt. Let apples sit for a few minutes.

Pour some soybean flour into a brown paper bag and shake a few apple rings at a time in the bag to give them a light coating of flour. This step helps the batter to stick during the frying process.

Beat the batter ingredients except oil together. Heat oil.

Dip the rings quickly into the batter and slide into the hot oil. Remove rings when they are puffy and lightly browned. Drain on paper towels.

VARIATIONS: Any leftover pancake or crêpe batter can be used in place of the batter given in this recipe. Pears may also be prepared this way.

## Soybean Crêpes
(*Makes 6 6-inch crêpes*)

Light and sunny yellow crêpes, these thin pancakes almost melt in your mouth.

3 eggs, beaten
½–⅔ cup water
⅓ cup soybean flour
1 tablespoon arrowroot flour starch
¼ teaspoon sea salt
2 tablespoons crushed sesame seeds
Sesame oil (for frying)

Beat all ingredients except oil together with a wire whisk. Heat a small cast-iron skillet. Test temperature with a drop of water; if it sizzles immediately, pan is ready. Brush pan with oil and pour in about 3 tablespoons batter. Tilt pan quickly to spread batter evenly.

Cook crêpes for about 4 minutes on each side, or until lightly browned. Stack on a plate and keep in a warm oven until ready to serve.

Serve with Apple Butter and sprinkle with cinnamon.

VARIATIONS: Add a scant teaspoon of grated lemon, orange, or tangerine rind to the batter. Orange or apple juice can be used in place of water.

## Yam Croquettes
*(Makes about 18 1-inch balls)*

An elegant way to get rid of holiday leftovers, this novel dessert makes the most of an often slighted vegetable.

3 medium-size yams
½ teaspoon sea salt
½ teaspoon cinnamon
½ teaspoon ground ginger
Dash of nutmeg
3 tablespoons chopped nuts
*Breading:*
⅓ cup rice flour
⅓ cup soy flour
½ cup whole-wheat pastry flour
¼ teaspoon sea salt
½ teaspoon cinnamon
1 quart oil for deep frying

Cook yams any way you prefer (bake, pressure-cook, steam, or boil). They should be soft in their jackets. Peel and purée the yams. Place purée in a saucepan with sea salt and cook over a low heat until purée is very thick. Chill purée for at least 1 hour. This may be done a day or two ahead of time, using leftover yams or sweet potatoes.

Mix spices and nuts into yam purée.

In a separate shallow pan, mix together breading mixture.

Heat oil in a deep skillet or wok.

To make croquettes, use a tablespoon as a measure, and scoop up a small amount of purée for each 1-inch sphere. Roll yam purée in breading. Make about 6 croquettes at a time and drop gently into the hot oil.

While the first batch is cooking, prepare another batch. Remove the first batch with a slotted spoon and drain on absorbent paper.

Repeat process until all of purée is used up. Croquettes may be kept warm in a low (250° F.) oven.

VARIATIONS: Cooked and puréed squash or carrots can be used in place of yams. Serve with chilled Soy Cream Sauce, Vanilla Sauce, or cold Tangy Applesauce.

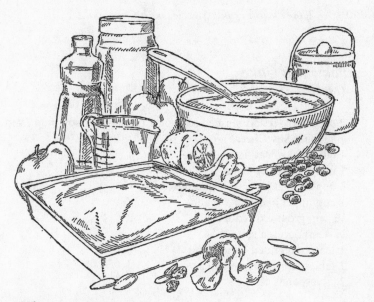

# Chapter 8. *Cakes*

The recipes developed for this chapter are not at all like the kinds of cakes you will find in pre-mixed packages purchased in the supermarket. These cakes are moist and sweet but not terribly light or fluffy. However, they are loaded with good things, and they complement any meal without anyone reaching for the Tums to soothe an upset tummy.

Cakes can be made with the simplest ingredients, and a good dessert doesn't have to be made with ultrarich ingredients in order to taste good. For health reasons, eggs, as well as oil, are kept to a minimum.

## Buckwheat Cake
(*Makes 8 servings*)

2 cups cooked and mashed soybeans (or leftover soy pulp from
    making Soy Cheese)
1 cup buckwheat flour
1 cup brown rice flour
3 apples, grated, or 1 cup applesauce
1 cup apple juice
½ cup ground dried fruit
½ teaspoon sea salt
1 teaspoon grated lemon rind
2 tablespoons sesame seeds
2 tablespoons oil
2 eggs

Preheat oven to 350° F.

Beat all ingredients together and pour into an oiled 9×12 inch
cake pan. Bake for 1 hour, or until top is firm and a toothpick inserted in the center comes out clean.

VARIATIONS: Add 1 teaspoon cinnamon and a dash of nutmeg.
Chopped nuts or ¼ cup Sesame Butter or Almond Butter can be
added to batter for a richer cake. Or, add 3 tablespoons carob
powder for a chocolate flavor.

## Carrot Cake
(*Makes 8 servings*)

If you own a juicer, you can substitute leftover carrot pulp for
the whole fresh carrots. Either way, this spicy orange-colored
cake is delicious.

1 pound carrots, grated
½ cup chestnut flour or Puréed Chestnuts
2 tablespoons soybean flour

½ cup flour (brown rice, barley, or whole-wheat pastry flour)
1 cup cooked grain (any cereal)
1 egg, optional
¼ cup sunflower or sesame oil
1½ cups liquid (grain coffee or fruit juice)
½ teaspoon each sea salt, ground cloves
2-inch piece of fresh gingerroot or 1 teaspoon ground ginger

Preheat oven to 350° F.

Mix well all ingredients except ginger. Peel gingerroot and finely grate. Squeeze out juice and discard pulp. Add juice to cake batter and beat thoroughly.

Pour batter into an oiled casserole or shallow cake pan and cover. Bake for 30 minutes, remove cover, and bake for another 20–30 minutes.

VARIATIONS: This cake can also be steamed in a pressure cooker. Place pan on a rack and have a 2-inch depth of water around pan. Bring up to full pressure. Lower flame and cook with medium pressure for 1 hour and 15 minutes. Let pressure fall normally. Add ½ cup raisins or currants for a sweeter flavor.

## Dutch Apple Cake
(*Makes 6–8 servings*)

1 cup whole-wheat pastry or unbleached white flour
¼ cup chestnut flour or soybean flour
¾ cup barley or oat flour
½ teaspoon cinnamon
¼ teaspoon sea salt
¼ cup sesame or safflower oil
1 cup apple juice or apple cider
1 vanilla bean
3 eggs, separated
2 tablespoons Sesame Butter or Almond Butter
4 large apples, cored and thinly sliced
¼ cup crushed nuts

Preheat oven to 350° F.

Sift dry ingredients into a bowl. Mix in oil and set aside. Simmer apple juice and vanilla bean in a covered saucepan for 10 minutes. Let cool. Remove bean.

Beat egg yolks until foamy. Beat the whites until they form soft peaks. Add apple juice and sesame butter to batter and beat until smooth. Beat in egg yolks and fold in egg whites.

Oil a 9×12 inch cake pan. Pour in half the batter and arrange a layer of apple slices on top. Repeat and cover with crushed nuts. Bake for 1 hour.


## Millet Cake
*(Makes one 9×5×3½ inch cake)*

Millet flour gives this cake the texture and taste of a rich poundcake—but without the calories of a cake made with lots of eggs and sugar.

1½ cups millet flour
½ cup sweet rice or brown rice flour
½ cup chestnut flour or Puréed Chestnuts
½ cup raisins or currants
2 cups apple juice
¼ cup sesame or safflower oil
¼ cup Sesame Butter or Nut Butter
½ teaspoon sea salt
½ teaspoon coriander
Dash of nutmeg, optional
½ cup roasted and chopped almonds

Preheat oven to 350° F.

Dry-roast flours in a cast-iron skillet for about 10 minutes, stirring constantly with a wooden spoon. If using puréed chestnuts, omit this step.

While millet and other flours are being roasted, simmer raisins in apple juice in a covered saucepan.

Purée raisins and liquid in a blender. Beat in remaining ingredients except for nuts. Fold in nuts and pour into an oiled 9×5×3½ inch bread pan and bake for 1 hour.

VARIATIONS: Cover bread with Sesame Glaze during the last 5 minutes of baking. For a chocolate marble cake effect, reduce apple juice to 1½ cups and swirl in ½ cup Carob Sauce mixed with 2 teaspoons dry carob powder.

## Millet Crunch Cake
(*Makes 8 servings*)

1 cup millet flour
½ cup chestnut or soybean flour
½ cup whole-wheat pastry flour or unbleached white flour
¼ teaspoon sea salt
¼ cup sesame or safflower oil
1½ cups apple cider
1 cup cooked grain (Puréed Rice Cream, couscous, or oatmeal)
1 egg
*Topping:*
2 teaspoons cinnamon
2 tablespoons Sesame Butter or Almond Butter
2 tablespoons sesame seeds
1 tablespoon oil
1 tablespoon fruit juice
½ cup chopped walnuts

Preheat oven to 350° F.

For cake combine dry ingredients. Add oil, liquid, and whole grain. Beat in egg. Pour batter into an oiled 9×12 inch cake pan.

Heat topping ingredients except nuts in a saucepan, adding more liquid if it is too stiff. Mix in nuts. Spread topping over cake and bake for 1 hour.

## Mock Cream Cheese Cake
*(Makes 6–8 servings)*

This recipe actually isn't an imitation of cream cheese cake, but a totally different recipe that just turns out tasting and looking like cream cheese cake. The secret ingredient is tofu, a soybean product.

1½ cups apple juice
½ cup chopped dried fruit
1 vanilla bean, split lengthwise
2 cups fresh Tofu or Soy Cheese*
⅓ cup Sesame Butter
½ cup sweet white rice flour
¼ teaspoon sea salt
1 teaspoon grated lemon or orange rind
*Crust:*
½ cup buckwheat flour
½ cup sweet brown rice flour
¼ cup whole-wheat pastry flour
4 tablespoons oil
1 teaspoon cinnamon
½ teaspoon sea salt
2 tablespoons crushed nuts or sesame seeds
¼ cup fruit juice

Preheat oven to 350° F.
Simmer together apple juice, fruit, and vanilla bean in a covered saucepan for 10 minutes. Remove vanilla bean and combine liquid in a blender with tofu. Add remaining ingredients of cake and blend again. Set aside.
Mix flours for crust and blend in oil with a fork. Add remaining ingredients and blend well. Crust will be crumbly. Reserve a few spoonfuls of crust and press remaining amount into a 9-inch pie pan. Bake crust for 10 minutes.

Remove crust and pour in filling. Sprinkle with reserved crust mixture. Bake for 40 minutes.

Serve pie chilled.

VARIATIONS: Serve with Fresh Fruit Glaze. This cake is also good served almost frozen—set pan in a freezer and remove when crystals begin to form around the edges.

---

* Tofu is a form of soybean curd sold in Oriental food stores. Tofu, or soy cheese, can also be made at home (see following recipe).

## *Tofu or Soy Cheese*
(*Makes about 2 cups*)

Soy products are high in protein but much lower in fat and calories than dairy products. Making your own cheese at home is not difficult and also is very inexpensive.

1 pound soybeans
4 cups water
A few yards of cheesecloth
3 tablespoons rice vinegar or lemon juice

Soak soybeans for 24 hours in water to cover, changing the water 3 times. Drain and grind the beans in a food mill or blender. Bring 4 cups fresh water to a boil with the ground beans. When the water comes to a boil add 1 more cup water. Bring to a boil again. Be careful—soy milk boils over, so stir with a spoon to prevent scorching and boiling over. Simmer milk for 20 minutes.

Strain milk through several layers of cheesecloth lining a fine strainer. Gather the corners of the cloth to make a sack and squeeze out excess liquid. The leftover pulp can be used in bread, cake, or cookie batters in place of whole cooked grain.

Place the liquid in a shallow glass container and add rice vinegar or lemon juice immediately. Let milk curdle. If curdling does not begin immediately, add a little more vinegar or lemon juice. Let soy milk stand for at least 2 hours in a warm place.

Strain through clean cloth again to remove excess liquid. Gather up sides of cloth and squeeze gently.

Place sack back into the strainer and rinse with cold water. Squeeze out liquid again. If you don't use soy cheese immediately, add a few grains of salt to cheese and store in an airtight container in the refrigerator. It will keep fresh for up to a week.

VARIATION: For quick soy milk, use 2 cups soybean flour and 8 cups cold water. Bring to a boil in a large pot and simmer for 20 minutes. Steps are identical for this method, but you should allow at least 3–4 hours for curdling to take place.

## Parsnip Banana Cake
### (*Makes 8–10 servings*)

Parsnips become incredibly sweet when cooked a long time, and in this recipe they resemble bananas in taste and texture.

3 pounds parsnips
2 tablespoons sesame oil
1 teaspoon sea salt
4 cups apple juice
1 vanilla bean or 1 teaspoon vanilla extract
1 lemon
1½ cups couscous
¼ cup Nut Butter

Scrub parsnips in cold water and slice into thin rounds. Heat oil in a pressure cooker or large skillet and sauté parsnips for 10 minutes. Add salt and 1 cup apple juice. Cover and cook for 45 minutes. If pressure cooking, cook under medium pressure for 20 minutes. Purée parsnips.

Preheat oven to 375° F.

Add remaining apple juice to parsnips and simmer in a covered pan with vanilla bean for 10 minutes. Remove vanilla bean. Grate lemon rind and add to parsnip mixture along with lemon juice. Mix in couscous and nut butter and transfer to an oiled casserole. Bake for 1 hour.

VARIATION: Add ½ teaspoon nutmeg and ½ cup chopped nuts to batter.

## Squash Spicecake
(*Makes 6–8 servings*)

Cooked squash can taste even sweeter than fruit. This cake has a rich color and retains its moisture throughout baking.

1 cup whole-wheat pastry flour
1 cup brown rice flour or barley flour
2 tablespoons soy flour
½ teaspoon sea salt
1 teaspoon coriander
1 teaspoon cinnamon
2 tablespoons poppy seeds
⅓ cup sesame or safflower oil
1 cup apple juice
¼ cup crushed walnuts
1 2-inch piece gingerroot or ½ teaspoon ginger powder
1 egg
2 cups cooked and puréed fall squash or yams
1 cup applesauce

Preheat oven to 350° F.

Mix dry ingredients. Blend oil with liquid and nuts. Peel gingerroot and finely grate. Squeeze out juice and discard pulp. Add ginger juice and remaining ingredients and beat by hand or use a blender.

Pour into an oiled 9×12×2½ inch cake pan and bake for 1 hour.

VARIATIONS: Strong dandelion or grain coffee can be used in place of the apple juice.

# Chapter 9. *Cookies and Crackers*

Almost everyone has fond memories associated with the wonderful aroma of warm cookies fresh from the oven. Cookies are practically foolproof—the batters are simple and easy to prepare. Included in this chapter are recipes to suit a variety of palates—two recipes for brownies made without chocolate, unusual recipes for wafers and light tea cookies, as well as fragrant fruit bars.

The recipes are designed for cookie and cracker doughs that don't need leavening agents. Unleavened cookies still turn out crunchy and chewy but don't spread out very much during baking. For this reason they should be flattened to the desired thickness before they are put in the oven to ensure uniform baking.

Cookies and crackers make great traveling companions, and most of the cookies included here keep well when stored in airtight containers.

## Aduki Brownies
*(Makes about 28 2-inch squares)*

These chewy brownies are made with high protein aduki beans, but they have the same appearance and similar taste of chocolate brownies.

1 cup uncooked aduki beans
3 cups apple juice or water
1 vanilla bean, split
1 cup Puréed Chestnuts
½ cup buckwheat flour or rye flour
1 cup whole-wheat pastry flour
½ teaspoon sea salt
1 teaspoon cinnamon
¼ cup sesame oil
1 egg
½ cup chopped nuts
½ to 1 cup chopped dates or currants, optional

Rinse aduki beans in cold water and sort out any foreign matter or spoiled beans. Place beans in pressure cooker with apple juice and vanilla bean and cook under full pressure for 45 minutes. If boiling, simmer beans in a covered saucepan for 2 hours.

Preheat oven to 350° F.

Remove vanilla bean and mash aduki beans until creamy. Blend in other ingredients. Pour batter into a well-oiled 9×15× 2½ inch cake pan. Bake for 1 hour and 15 minutes, or until the top is dark and firm to the touch. Cut into approximately 28 squares.

## Amasake Cookies

(*Makes 3 dozen small cookies*)

2 cups Amasake
1 cup whole-wheat pastry flour or unbleached white flour
1 cup oat flakes
¼ teaspoon sea salt
¼ cup crushed nuts or sesame seeds

Preheat oven to 375° F. and insert cookie sheet.

Combine all ingredients and mix well. Amasake is very wet; however, if batter appears to be very stiff, add a little water. Batter should have the consistency of a thick muffin batter.

Remove cookie sheet from oven and brush with oil. Using a wet spoon, drop dough onto pan; flatten with the tines of a fork. Bake for 15 minutes.

VARIATIONS: Wheat flakes or bran can be used in place of the oat flakes. Chopped almonds are especially good in this recipe, as well as chopped dried fruit. For spicy cookies, add ½ teaspoon each ground cinnamon, cloves, and coriander.


## Barley Cookies

(*Makes 2 dozen 2-inch cookies*)

This light tea cookie is almost like a cracker. It stores well in an airtight container.

1½ cups barley flour
½ cup buckwheat flour
½ cup chestnut flour or sweet rice flour
¼ cup roasted sesame seeds
¼ teaspoon sea salt
2 tablespoons sesame or sunflower seed oil
1½ cups apple juice
1 teaspoon cinnamon

Preheat oven to 350° F.

Using a dry cast-iron skillet, pan-roast the flours over a medium flame until they give off a nutty fragrance. Stir constantly to prevent burning. Pour flour into a bowl and let cool.

Mix flours, seeds, and salt together. Add oil, rubbing it into the dough with your fingers to make a mealy consistency. Add liquid, a small amount at a time. As soon as the dough becomes soft and holds together, stop adding liquid and knead for about 5 minutes. Then pinch off pieces of dough and roll into 1-inch balls. Brush cookie sheet with oil and press dough onto surface with the tines of a moistened fork. Flatten out each ball to a 2-inch diameter. Sprinkle with cinnamon. Bake for 20 minutes.


## Buckwheat Cookies
(*Makes about 5 dozen*)

1 cup roasted buckwheat groats
1 cup chopped dried fruit
4 cups fruit juice or water
½ teaspoon sea salt
½ cup chestnut or soybean flour
½ cup brown rice flour
½ cup whole-wheat pastry flour
1 cup toasted oat flakes
½ cup roasted sesame seeds

Preheat oven to 350° F.

In a 2-quart saucepan, bring buckwheat groats, fruit, and liquid to a boil. Add salt, reduce flame, and cover pan. Simmer for 15 minutes. Let cool for 15 minutes.

Combine all ingredients in a mixing bowl except for oat flakes and sesame seeds. Form dough into small balls (it helps to dip your fingers in cold water), then roll first in sesame seeds and then the oat flakes. Oil a cookie sheet and place balls 1 inch apart. Press down with the tines of a moistened fork and bake for 15 minutes.

## Carob Brownies
(*Makes 28 2-inch squares*)

½ cup carob powder
2 cups apple juice
1 vanilla bean, split lengthwise
1 cup whole-wheat pastry flour or unbleached white flour
½ cup buckwheat flour or rye flour
2 tablespoons soybean flour
1 cup Puréed Chestnuts, optional
½ teaspoon sea salt
½ teaspoon coriander
½ cup chopped nuts
½ cup currants or chopped dates
¼ cup sesame oil plus extra oil for cake pan
1 egg

Preheat oven to 350° F.

Place carob powder in a saucepan. Beat in apple juice with a wire whisk. Bring to a boil and drop in vanilla bean. Simmer uncovered for 15 minutes, stirring occasionally to prevent burning. Remove vanilla bean and set liquid aside to cool.

Combine all ingredients together in a mixing bowl. Pour batter into a well-oiled 9×15×2½ inch cake pan. Bake for 1 hour and 15 minutes, or until the top is dark and firm to the touch. Cut into 28 2-inch squares.

## Chestnut Bran Wafers
(*Makes 3½ dozen 3-inch cookies*)

2 cups oat flakes
1 tablespoon sesame oil
2 cups wheat bran or rice bran
3 cups liquid (grain coffee, fruit juice, etc.)
2 cups cooked grain (any cereal)
1 vanilla bean, split lengthwise
½ teaspoon sea salt
1 teaspoon cinnamon
1 cup Puréed Chestnuts

In a dry cast-iron skillet, pan-roast the oat flakes, stirring constantly to prevent burning. As soon as they become golden, remove and pour into a large mixing bowl. Add oil to skillet, return to flame, and sauté the bran, stirring constantly for 5–10 minutes. Add to the toasted oat flakes.

In a separate pan, bring liquid, cooked grain, vanilla bean, and salt to a boil. Cover and simmer for 15 minutes.

Preheat oven to 375° F. Place a food mill or fine sieve over the oat-bran mixture and pour through the cooked grain mixture. Remove vanilla bean and purée the grain into the bowl. Add any leftover bran that remains in the mill to the batter.

Beat well. Add cinnamon and puréed chestnuts and mix thoroughly. Brush a cookie sheet with oil and drop dough onto sheet in large spoonfuls. Batter should be very soft and wet. Bake for 35–40 minutes.

## Corn Pretzels and Crackers
(*Makes 6 dozen*)

These crackers are a terrific party food and taste much better than any store-bought variety.

4 cups pan-roasted corn flour
4 cups boiling water
1 tablespoon sea salt
1 cup whole-wheat pastry flour
1 cup chestnut flour, or
⅓ cup soybean flour plus ⅔ cup brown rice flour
1 cup toasted sesame seeds
Oil

Preheat oven to 400° F.
Pour corn flour into a large mixing bowl. Scald corn flour with water, and stir well. When all the corn flour is moistened, add salt. Let cool for at least 10 minutes before adding remaining flours.

Knead dough for 10 minutes. To make crackers, spread a thin layer of sesame seeds out on a cookie sheet. Divide dough into 3 sections and roll out 1 section directly on cookie sheet. (I generally use a glass or small wooden pestle to smooth the dough out in the corners of the cookie sheet.) Sprinkle the top of the dough with more seeds. Now, use a glass or small rolling pin and, pressing down against the dough, force the seeds into dough as you roll. Wet a knife and score the dough into squares or triangles and punch holes in each cracker with a fork to allow for steam to escape. This is very important, because otherwise the crackers will puff up in some places and crack during baking. Bake in oven for 12 minutes.

If you want to deep-fry the crackers, prepare the same way as above. Drop cut crackers into hot oil and remove as soon as they float to the top of oil and are lightly browned.

For pretzels, break off sections of dough and roll them into long strips, about ½ inch in diameter. Break off every 6 inches, or leave strips slightly longer for fancy pretzels. Roll strips in sesame seeds. Loop the ends loosely and squeeze ends together. This is the best part of making crackers. Join 2 circles for figure eights, or twist the circles into any shape desired. Drop pretzels into hot oil and remove when they swell and float to the top of the oil and turn golden brown. The pretzels may also be baked as the crackers.

This recipe does make an enormous amount of crackers, but it seems ridiculous to make a small amount because otherwise they will all be eaten up before you are through cooking them.

If you don't feel like using up all the dough at one time, wrap it tightly in waxed paper and store in the refrigerator. The crackers and pretzels that are baked will keep for up to a week. Fried crackers and pretzels should be used up in a day or two.

## Corn Sesame Crunchies
### (*Makes about 30 2-inch squares*)

These cookies were made originally by a natural food company in Belgium. When they were no longer available in this country, I experimented until I reached a pretty good imitation.

⅔ cup currants or chopped dried fruit
2 cups fruit juice
⅔ cup corn flour
⅓ cup soybean flour
1 cup whole-wheat pastry flour
½ cup brown rice flour or barley flour
1 egg, optional
¼ cup sunflower or sesame seed oil
1 teaspoon cinnamon
½ teaspoon sea salt
1 cup sesame seeds, lightly toasted

Preheat oven to 375° F.

Bring currants and fruit juice to a boil in a saucepan and simmer for 5 minutes. Pour corn flour into a mixing bowl and, holding a strainer over bowl, scald corn flour with cooking liquid. Mix thoroughly.

Purée the cooked fruit in a blender or food mill. Add to corn flour and mix in remaining ingredients.

Oil a shallow cake pan or cookie sheet and spread out batter with a spatula to about ½-inch thickness. Bake for 15–20 minutes. Cut into squares while cookies are still warm. Crunchies will keep crisp and fresh for about a week in an airtight container.

## Cracked Wheat Cookies
(*Makes about 3 dozen 2-inch cookies*)

If you like the sweet taste of cracked wheat cereal, you'll probably find these cookies especially appealing.

1 cup cooked cracked wheat or bulgur
1 cup whole-wheat pastry flour
½ cup rye flour or buckwheat flour
¼ cup soybean flour or chestnut flour
¼ cup chopped nuts or sunflower seeds
¼ cup vegetable oil
¾ cup fruit juice
1 teaspoon cinnamon
½ teaspoon coriander
½ teaspoon sea salt

Preheat oven to 350° F.

Mix all ingredients well in a large bowl. Knead for a few minutes. Form dough into small balls. Place balls on an oiled cookie sheet and press down with a wet fork. The thinner the dough, the crisper the cookies will be.

Bake for 15–20 minutes. These cookies are light and crunchy and good to take on trips. The top may be glazed with fruit butter during the last 5 minutes of baking for a sweeter cookie.

VARIATION: Cracked rye cereal may be used in place of wheat for great crunchy cookies.

## Fruit Bars
(*Makes about 24 bars*)

Chewy, fragrant, and sweet, these fruit bars are a great finger food because they hold together so well.

1 cup chopped dates, figs, or prunes
½ cup currants
1 cup strong mu tea or sassafras tea
½ cup fruit juice
Juice and grated rind of 1 lemon
2 cups toasted oat flakes
½ cup bran
1 cup whole-wheat pastry flour
½ teaspoon sea salt
1 teaspoon cinnamon
½ cup chopped nuts or sunflower seeds
¼ cup toasted sesame seeds

Preheat oven to 350° F.

Simmer the dried fruit, currants, and liquid together for 5 minutes. Pour into a mixing bowl and mix in remaining ingredients. Oil a cookie sheet and press dough out to about ½-inch thickness.

Bake for 40 minutes. Cool for at least 30 minutes before cutting into bars.

VARIATIONS: One or 2 eggs can be added to the batter for lighter bars. Orange juice and rind can be used in place of lemon. Keep bars in an airtight container in the refrigerator to keep fresh.

## Lemon Drops
*(Makes 3 dozen wafers)*

These are light and delicate cookies subtly flavored with lemon.

3 cups sweet brown rice flour or regular brown rice flour
1½ cups Amasake
½ teaspoon sea salt
¼ cup sesame or sunflower oil
¼ cup roasted sesame seeds
1 apple, grated
1 lemon (use all of the grated rind and juice)

Preheat oven to 350° F. and insert cookie sheets.

Mix all ingredients together. Roll dough into small balls. Remove cookie sheets and brush with oil. Press dough onto sheets and press down with the tines of a wet fork until diameter is about 2½ inches and dough is ⅛ inch thick.

Bake for 10 minutes, then turn cookies over with a spatula and bake for another 5 minutes.

VARIATIONS: Use an orange or tangerine in place of the lemon. Add 1 teaspoon crushed anise seeds for an entirely different flavor.

## Granola Cookies
*(Makes about 24 2-inch squares)*

These are very sweet crunchy cookies, and they store well when kept in airtight glass jars.

3 cups Super Granola
1 cup whole-wheat pastry flour
¼ cup soybean flour
1 cup boiling liquid (fruit juice, grain coffee, or mu tea)
¼ cup Amasake Syrup or barley malt extract
1 teaspoon sea salt
½ cup chopped walnuts
½ cup chopped dried fruit

Preheat oven to 350° F.
Combine all ingredients in a mixing bowl. Mix batter well, and let it sit for about 10 minutes.
Oil a cookie sheet and spread batter out with a spatula. Score into 2-inch squares, using a wet knife. Bake for 30–40 minutes.

## Oatmeal Cookies
*(Makes about 3 dozen 2½-inch cookies)*

Light and nutritious oatmeal cookies are always a favorite. This recipe is unique in that only a minimum of flour is used.

3 cups oat flakes
2 cups boiling fruit juice
½ cup chestnut flour, or
   ¼ cup each soybean flour and rice flour
½ cup whole-wheat pastry flour
¼ cup chopped walnuts or sunflower seeds
2 tablespoons sesame seeds
2 tablespoons oil

½ teaspoon sea salt
1 teaspoon cinnamon
1 teaspoon vanilla or almond extract
½ cup chopped dates or figs

Preheat oven to 375° F.

Pan-roast the oat flakes in a dry cast-iron skillet, stirring constantly, until they are golden in color. Pour flakes into a mixing bowl and scald with hot liquid. Let flakes sit for about 5–10 minutes to absorb liquid.

Beat in remaining ingredients. Brush a cookie sheet with oil, drop batter using a tablespoon, and flatten with a wet fork. Bake for 15–20 minutes.

VARIATION: To make oat bars, oil cookie sheet and spread out batter with a spatula. Bake for 25–30 minutes and cut into bars while still warm.

## Peanut Butter Bars
*(Makes about 28 2-inch bars)*

Batter for Oatmeal Cookies
1 cup natural peanut butter (not hydrogenated)
1 egg
½ teaspoon coriander

Preheat oven to 375° F.

Mix all ingredients together and spread out on an oiled cookie sheet with a spatula. Bake for 25–30 minutes and cut into bars while still warm.

VARIATIONS: Use 1 cup Valencia peanuts and omit chopped nuts and sesame seeds. For carob-peanut butter bars, replace ¼ cup of the whole-wheat pastry flour with carob flour.

## Peanut Butter Wafers
*(Makes 3 dozen)*

These light wafers practically melt in your mouth.

3 cups wheat bran or rice bran
1½ cups natural peanut butter (not hydrogenated)
1 cup cooked grain (rice, couscous, or oatmeal)
1 teaspoon cinnamon
1 tablespoon dry Pero (a grain coffee substitute)

Preheat oven to 375° F.

Pan-roast the bran in a dry skillet, stirring constantly until it darkens slightly. Pour the bran into a mixing bowl. Using a wooden spoon or rubber spatula, work the peanut butter into the bran and add other ingredients, mixing thoroughly. Dough should be fairly stiff but easy to knead.

Wetting your hands frequently with cold water, pinch off pieces of dough and roll into balls about 1 inch in diameter.

Oil a cookie sheet and place balls 3 inches apart. Using a moistened fork, make a crisscross pattern by pressing the tines deeply into the dough.

Bake for about 12 minutes. These cookies are extremely light and flaky.


## Whole-Wheat Crackers
*(Makes 24 2-inch squares)*

These crackers store nicely in an airtight canister. They are crisp and can be used with dips or spreads.

2 cups cooked cracked wheat or any other cracked cereal
1 cup whole-wheat pastry flour
½ cup corn flour or millet flour

2 tablespoons soybean flour
2 tablespoons chestnut flour, optional
½ teaspoon sea salt
1 teaspoon cinnamon or coriander
2 tablespoons sesame or poppy seeds

Preheat oven to 400° F.

Knead all ingredients together except seeds. Dough should be firm, but if too stiff, add a little water. Dough can either be rolled out on a well-floured bread board and cut into triangles, circles, etc., or rolled out directly on an oiled cookie sheet. Score the sheet with a wet knife and sprinkle dough with seeds. Prick tiny holes in crackers with a fork to allow steam to escape. Bake for 15 minutes.

VARIATIONS: To add more flavor to this plain dough, try adding lemon, orange, or tangerine rind. Caraway or anise seeds can be used in place of sesame seeds for an exotic flavor.

# Chapter 10. *Pastries*

Pastries made from unrefined grains and oils can be just as light and flaky as the store-bought bakery products. You will find that whole grain flours are sweeter than bleached or enriched flours because they retain their natural oils. Also, oat, barley, and sweet brown rice flours are used in combination with whole-wheat flour to make lighter doughs.

Oil has been cut down to a minimum throughout this chapter, but if you prefer richer-tasting dough, add a little more oil to suit your needs.

For best results in making flaky doughs, chill the oil and use very cold water. Don't knead the dough too much—excess kneading brings out the gluten, which can make a pastry dough very tough.

## Deep-Dish Apple Pie
(*Makes about 9 servings*)

Nothing is more familiar to us than old-fashioned apple pie. This recipe incorporates a flaky oat crust with a rich golden color.

8 large apples (a combination of golden delicious and red
    apples works best)
1 cup apple cider
1 heaping tablespoon arrowroot flour starch or kuzu
¼ teaspoon sea salt
½ teaspoon cinnamon
1 tablespoon lemon juice
½ cup currants or raisins
1 tablespoon grated lemon or orange rind
¼ cup lightly roasted corn meal or wheat germ
Oat Flake Piecrust (recipe follows) or Whole-Wheat Piecrust

Preheat oven to 375° F.
Wash, core, and peel apples and cut into eighths. Bring cider, arrowroot, salt, cinnamon, and lemon juice to a boil. Add raisins. Simmer for 1 minute. Add lemon rind and apples and remove from heat.
Coat the bottom of a deep casserole with corn meal. Spoon in apple filling and cover with oat crust. Prick dough to allow steam to escape. Bake for 45 minutes.
VARIATIONS: Serve with Vanilla Sauce or Soy Cream Sauce.

## Oat Flake Piecrust
   (*Makes 1 thick crust*)

Many people like the taste of this crust so much that I usually bake an extra crust sans filling for munching.

   1½ cups oat flakes
   ¾ cup brown rice flour
   ½ teaspoon sea salt
   ⅓ cup cold oil
   1 teaspoon cinnamon
   1 egg, optional
   2–3 tablespoons cold water or fruit juice
   2 tablespoons crushed nuts or seeds

Mix together first 5 ingredients. Dough should be very crumbly. Add egg and a small amount of water. As soon as dough begins to hold together stop adding water.

Dough will be very soft and doesn't need to be rolled out. For a bottom crust, simply press dough into a pie pan with your fingers. For a top crust, crumble over pie filling.

Use leftover crust as a cookie dough by adding chopped nuts or fruit and bake at the same time as you make the pie.

## Unyeasted Donuts
   (*Makes 3½ dozen*)

   2 cups whole-wheat pastry flour
   ½ cup chestnut flour
   ½ cup rice flour, barley flour, or oat flour
   ¼ teaspoon sea salt
   1 cup apple cider
   Extra flour for rolling donuts
   Vegetable oil for deep frying

Mix first 5 ingredients. Batter should be moist and similar to bread dough. Cover with a damp cloth and let sit overnight or longer to ferment slightly. Roll dough out on flour and cut with a donut cutter or form into loops. Deep-fry until puffed and lightly browned. Remove with a strainer and drain on paper towels.

NOTE: If you're in a hurry and don't mind using eggs, replace some of the apple cider with a beaten egg or two.

VARIATIONS: You can add any spice you like to the dough. Add a tablespoon or two of soybean flour for a richer-tasting batter.

Glaze donuts with Carob Sauce, Apple Butter, or Sesame Glaze.

## *Yeasted Donuts*
*(Makes 18–24 donuts, depending on size)*

½ teaspoon dry yeast
½ cup warm water
2 cups whole-wheat pastry flour
1 cup sweet brown rice flour
¼ cup soybean flour
¾ teaspoon sea salt
1 teaspoon cinnamon
½ teaspoon coriander, optional
2 tablespoons corn or sesame oil
1 or 2 eggs
2 cups apple juice
½ teaspoon grated lemon rind
Extra flour for rolling donuts
Oil for deep frying

Add yeast to warm water in a bowl and let soften. In a separate bowl, mix dry ingredients; blend in oil.

Beat egg, juice, and lemon rind into yeast. Add liquids to dry ingredients, knead well, and cover with a damp cloth. Place in a warm spot (about 75–80° F.) and allow to double in size.

Roll dough out on a well-floured board to ½-inch thickness. Cut donuts into desired shape and cover. Place in a warm spot and let rise for at least another 30 minutes.

Deep-fry in enough oil for donuts to float freely to the top of the oil (about 3 inches depth in the center of the pan). Remove with a slotted spoon and drain on paper towels.

## *Fruit Crisp*
(*Makes 6 generous servings*)

⅓ cup whole-wheat pastry flour
2½ cups toasted oat flakes
1 tablespoon soybean flour
1 teaspoon cinnamon
½ teaspoon sea salt
⅓ cup sesame, safflower, or sunflower seed oil
1 orange
6 large apples (or pears, peaches, etc.), cored and sliced into
　eighths
½ cup chopped dried fruit
½ cup chopped walnuts or almonds

Preheat oven to 375° F.

Mix dry ingredients together in a bowl. Add oil and rub into mixture with your fingers until crumbly. Cut the orange in half and squeeze juice over the oat mixture. Grate a little orange rind in too if you want a little extra bite.

Press about ⅓ of the oat mixture into a shallow cake pan. Arrange a layer of apples and some of the dried fruit and nuts. Repeat until all the apples and oat crumbs are used up. Cover pan tightly with foil.

Bake for 40 minutes. Remove cover and place under the broiler for a few minutes until the top is brown.

VARIATIONS: Stewed prunes or apricots can be used in place of fresh fruit. Or, try blueberries or pitted cherries.

## Fruit Pie
*(Makes 6–8 servings)*

This is a basic recipe for any fresh ripe fruit, such as apples, apricots, peaches, pears, plums, or figs.

3–4 pounds fresh fruit
1 cup apple cider
¼ teaspoon sea salt
1 heaping tablespoon arrowroot starch flour
½ teaspoon cinnamon
Dash of nutmeg
1 tablespoon lemon juice
1–2 tablespoons Amasake Syrup or barley malt extract
Whole-Wheat Piecrust (recipe follows)

Preheat oven to 350° F.
Rinse and core fruit if needed. Peeling skins is unnecessary if you're using organically grown fruit. Combine all ingredients in a large, heavy saucepan. Bring to a boil and simmer for 10 minutes.
Bake piecrust for 10 minutes. Remove from heat and spoon in filling. Bake for 45 minutes.
This recipe calls for only a bottom crust, but if you like a little crust on the top, cut leftover pie dough into thin strips and make a lattice effect by crisscrossing them over the top of filling. Or, just sprinkle some wheat germ on the top of the pie for a light topping.

## *Whole-Wheat Piecrust*

(*Makes 1 generous crust*)

1 cup whole-wheat pastry flour or unbleached white flour
1 cup whole-wheat flour
¼ teaspoon sea salt
⅓–½ cup cold oil
½ teaspoon cinnamon
1 tablespoon grated lemon or orange rind
⅓ cup ice water
2 tablespoons crushed nuts or seeds

Combine flours and salt in a mixing bowl. Add oil and mix with your fingers or a fork until mixture resembles fine meal. Add remaining ingredients and knead gently, just until mixture begins to form a ball. If using ½ cup oil, decrease amount of water, or dough will be too soft. Pie dough should be somewhat flaky for best results.

Roll dough out on a floured board and transfer to pie pan.

VARIATION: Add the yolk of an egg for a richer dough.

## *Uses for Leftover Pie Dough*

PIGS IN BLANKET:

Quarter an apple or pear. Sprinkle fruit with a little salt and dust with cinnamon and wrap in thin pieces of dough. Bake for 20 minutes in a 375° F. oven. You can use whole dried figs or dates in place of fresh fruit.

FRIED PUFFS:

Roll dough very thin. Cut into triangles, rounds, etc., and deep-fry. Very light and rich.

## Lemon Meringue Pie
(*Makes 6–8 servings*)

*Filling:*
4 tablespoons arrowroot flour starch
4 tablespoons unbleached white flour or sweet rice flour
½ cup cold apple juice
⅛ teaspoon sea salt
1¼ cups boiling apple juice
½ cup Amasake Syrup, Fruit Syrup, or ¼ cup barley malt
   extract
3 egg yolks, well beaten
Rind and juice of 2 lemons
1 tablespoon corn oil
*Meringue:*
3 egg whites
Dash of salt
1 tablespoon Amasake Syrup or barley malt extract
*Crust:*
Whole-Wheat Piecrust, baked for 10 minutes

Preheat oven to 350° F.
Mix together arrowroot and flour in ½ cup cold apple juice in
a saucepan. Add salt, boiling apple juice, and syrup, beating well
with a whisk, and cook over a double boiler or asbestos pad for
10 minutes. Beat in egg yolks rapidly, then add lemon rind and
juice and oil. Remove from heat and let cool.
   Beat together egg whites, salt, and syrup until stiff. Pour filling
into baked crust, top with meringue, and bake for 10–15 minutes,
or until meringue is lightly browned.
   VARIATION: If you would rather not use egg yolks, substitute
Lemon Cream Custard for the filling.

# *Parsnip Pie*
### (*Makes 6–8 servings*)

Strange as it may sound, onions and parsnips combined create a very sweet and satisfying pie filling.

3 pounds fresh parsnips
1 pound white onions
1 tablespoon sesame oil
½ cup water or apple juice
½ teaspoon sea salt
2 tablespoons Sesame Butter
1 teaspoon cinnamon
¼ teaspoon nutmeg

CRUST:

¾ cup oat flakes
½ cup barley flour or brown rice flour
½ cup corn flour
1 teaspoon cinnamon
1 tablespoon grated lemon or orange rind
½ teaspoon sea salt
⅓ cup safflower oil
1 tablespoon fruit juice

Scrub the parsnips thoroughly and slice on the diagonal into thin rounds. Peel onions and cut into thin slivers. Heat oil in a cast-iron skillet and sauté the onions for a few minutes. Add parsnips and sauté for about 5 more minutes, stirring gently. Add water, cover pan, and cook over low heat for 20 minutes. Add salt and cook for another 20 minutes.

Preheat oven to 350° F.

In a mixing bowl, combine all ingredients for piecrust except oil and fruit juice. Mix oil in with a fork. The dough should be very crumbly. Mix in fruit juice. Press dough into a 9-inch pie pan, reserving a few spoonfuls for pie topping.

Bake piecrust for 10 minutes. Remove from oven and set aside.

Purée cooked parsnips and onions and blend in sesame butter and spices. Pile filling into crust, sprinkle with reserved topping mixture, and bake for 35 minutes.

Serve warm or chilled.

## Strudel
*(Makes 2 5×12 inch rolls)*

Almost every country seems to have its own version of strudel—a rich dessert made of flaky layers of dough wrapped around a sweet filling. Because it is so delightfully rich, you will probably want to serve it cut into thin slices. This basic recipe is very flexible and allows for a variety of different preparations.

UNYEASTED DOUGH (recipe for yeasted dough follows):

4 cups whole-wheat pastry flour
⅔ cup sesame or sunflower oil plus ¼ cup extra oil
¾ teaspoon sea salt
1 teaspoon cinnamon
1 tablespoon grated orange, lemon, or tangerine rind
½ to 1 cup ice cold apple juice

FILLING:

4 cups Fresh Fruit Glaze or Dried Fruit Purée, or see other
    fillings below

1 beaten egg yolk (for glaze)
⅓ cup crushed nuts or sesame seeds
¼ cup corn meal for baking sheet

Mix first 5 ingredients together in a large mixing bowl and rub with your fingers or a pastry blender until it resembles a fine meal. Add juice gradually and gently knead; stop adding juice when the dough begins to pull away from the sides of the bowl.

Knead until the dough is soft and pliable. Divide dough in half. Roll out each section on a well-floured bread board. If using yeasted dough, the steps from here on are identical.

Roll out the dough into a rectangle as thin as possible. Using a pastry brush, oil the entire surface of the dough. Fold dough in half, with oiled section inside. Roll out again and repeat process. This will make a very flaky crust. Repeat for other section of dough.

For the last rolling, form a rectangle about 12×15 inches. Cover each rectangle with 2 cups of filling, leaving a 1-inch border on all sides. Fold dough over twice, as if you were folding a letter. Seal edges closed with wet fingers.

Preheat over to 350° F. Let strudel dough rest on top of stove for about 20 minutes.

Brush strudels with egg yolks (for a nice golden finish) and sprinkle with seeds or nuts. Make a few slashes with a sharp knife or razor to allow steam to escape during baking. Place on a cookie sheet coated with corn meal and bake for 40 minutes for yeasted strudel, 50 minutes for unyeasted strudel.

YEASTED DOUGH:

2 cups unbleached white or pastry flour
1 cup whole-wheat flour
½ teaspoon dry yeast, softened for 10 minutes in a little warm
   water
½ teaspoon sea salt
1 teaspoon cinnamon
½ cup sesame oil plus ¼ cup extra oil
½ cup apple juice
1–2 cups extra flour

Mix all ingredients together in a ceramic or glass bowl (except for extra flour) and stir well. Cover bowl with damp cloth and let dough rise in a warm place for about 2 hours.

Punch dough down and add flour until dough is soft and pliable. Return to bowl, cover, and let rise until doubled in bulk.

FILLING VARIATIONS:

*Poppy Seed Filling:*

Add ½ cup washed and gently roasted poppy seeds to Fresh
Fruit Glaze or Dried Fruit Purée.

*Apple Filling:*
½ cup apple butter
2 cups sliced apples
½ cup currants
½ cup chopped nuts
1 teaspoon cinnamon
¼ cup nut butter

Mix all ingredients together and spread over dough.

*Chestnut filling:*
3 cups Puréed Chestnuts
½ cup chopped nuts
½ cup apple butter

Mix all ingredients together and spread over dough.


## Stuffed Pastries
(*Makes about 2 dozen 3½-inch pastries*)

Strudel dough
4 cups any filling
Beaten egg yolk for glaze

Preheat oven to 350° F.
Roll out strudel dough. Cut into triangles, circles, or squares.
Place a small amount of filling in the center of dough and fold
sides over. Prick edges to seal with the tines of a wet fork
and flute the edges by making small pinches with your thumb and

forefinger. Poke a few holes in the top with a toothpick or fork and place on an oiled cookie sheet. Brush with beaten egg yolks. Bake for 30–40 minutes.

## *Cinnamon Rolls*
*(Makes about 2 dozen rolls)*

Follow directions for making either yeasted or unyeasted strudel dough. For filling, mix together 2 tablespoons cinnamon, 1 cup fruit or apple butter, and ½ cup chopped nuts. Spread filling over dough and make a jelly roll. Cut roll into 1-inch sections and place spiral side up on a well-oiled cake pan.

Preheat oven to 350° F.

Bake for 30–40 minutes.

## *Vegetarian Mincemeat pie*
*(Makes about 9 servings)*

This is a richly flavored impostor of the traditional holiday favorite.

½ cup aduki beans
½ cup raisins or currants
1 cup dried apples
½ cup dried pears
4–5 cups water
1 teaspoon cinnamon
½ teaspoon ground ginger
½ teaspoon sea salt
½ cup chopped walnuts
2 tablespoons Nut Butter
Rye or Whole-Wheat Piecrust

Place beans, dried fruit, water, and cinnamon in a large, heavy saucepan or pressure cooker. If pressure cooking, use only 4 cups of water. Pressure-cook for 45 minutes once pressure goes up. For regular cooking, use 5 cups of water, bring ingredients to a boil, and then cover, lower flame, and simmer for 2 hours.

Preheat oven to 350° F.

Prepare piecrust and place in a 9-inch-diameter pan. Bake for 10 minutes and remove from oven.

Purée aduki bean filling and mix in remaining ingredients. Spoon into piecrust and cover with thin strips of leftover pie dough. Bake for 40 minutes.

VARIATION: Cooked chestnuts can be used in place of walnuts.


## Yam Cream Pie
(*Makes 6–8 servings*)

2 pounds yams
2-inch piece of gingerroot
2 cups Puréed Rice Cream, Amasake, or cooked oatmeal
4 tablespoons Sesame Butter or Nut Butter
¼ teaspoon sea salt (omit if sesame butter is salted)
½ cup pecans (reserve a couple for garnish), finely chopped
Baked Buckwheat Piecrust (see below)

Steam, pressure-cook, or bake yams until soft in their jackets. Cool, then peel and mash. Peel gingerroot and finely grate. Squeeze out the juice and discard the pulp. Preheat oven to 375° F.

Mix all ingredients together until filling is smooth and creamy. Pour yam filling into piecrust and top with remaining pecans.

Bake for 30 minutes. Serve hot or cold.

## *Buckwheat Piecrust*

½ cup buckwheat flour
½ cup sweet brown rice flour or brown rice flour
¼ cup whole-wheat pastry flour
2 tablespoons crushed seeds or nuts
⅓ cup sunflower or safflower oil
½ teaspoon sea salt
½ teaspoon cinnamon, optional
Few tablespoons cold water

Preheat oven to 375° F.

Combine dry ingredients in a bowl and rub oil into flours with your fingers. Add just enough water so that dough holds together, but it should remain crumbly. Press into a 9-inch pie pan and bake for 15 minutes.

The beauty of this simple pie dough is that it resembles a graham cracker crust and it doesn't have to be rolled out! It holds up especially well under creamy fillings and puddings. Or, you can use the dough as a topping for fruit desserts by simply crumbling cooked pie dough over applesauce, fresh or dried stewed fruit, etc.

## *Yam Applesauce Pie*
(*Makes 6–8 servings*)

2 pounds yams
2-inch piece of gingerroot
½ teaspoon sea salt
Arrowroot flour starch (about 1 tablespoon)
½ cup fruit juice
Baked Oat Flake or Whole-Wheat Piecrust
2 cups applesauce

Prepare the yams and gingerroot as in Yam Cream Pie. Preheat oven to 375° F. In a saucepan combine sea salt, arrowroot, and juice and mix until a thin paste. Add puréed yams and cook over a low flame, stirring constantly, until thick. Add ginger juice to filling and pour into crust. Cover with applesauce and bake for 20 minutes.

Serve warm or cold. Garnish with crushed nuts if desired.

## Corn Meal Piecrust
*(Makes 1 crust)*

½ cup corn flour
½ cup boiling water
⅓ cup oil
¼ teaspoon sea salt
1½ cups whole-wheat pastry flour
1 egg, optional

Scald the corn flour with boiling water. Add oil and beat with a fork for a few minutes to blend. Add salt and flour. Beat in egg. Refrigerate dough for a few hours before rolling.

This is a rich-tasting flaky crust that goes especially well with squash or Pumpkin Pie Filling.

## Rye Piecrust
*(Makes about 2 8-inch crusts)*

1½ cups rye flour
2½ cups whole-wheat pastry flour
¾ cup oil
½ teaspoon sea salt
1 tablespoon poppy seeds, optional
⅓ cup ice water

Combine all ingredients except water until fine and crumbly. Add water gradually and stop when dough begins to pull away from sides of bowl. Knead gently and roll out on a well-floured board.

VARIATIONS: Rice flour, barley flour, or oat flour can be used in place of rye.

# Chapter 11. *Puddings and Gelatins*

Creamy, rich-tasting puddings and custards can be prepared without those high calorie-laden ingredients. Natural whole grain products can be used most advantageously to produce pleasing textures, and when combined with fruits, spices, and nut butters, the results are surprisingly similar to desserts made with heavy cream and refined sugar.

Hearty puddings chock full of fruits and nuts and topped with sauces are most welcome in the colder weather when served still warm. In warm weather, light, airy puddings served well chilled or almost frozen are always refreshing desserts.

Agar-agar (or kanten) is used in place of regular gelatin, which is an animal byproduct. Agar-agar is a clear vegetable gelatin; colorless and odorless, it is full of minerals and has almost no fat and very little carbohydrate value. It lends itself very well to endless variations of cooked puddings and gelatins.

There are several important items to remember when using this type of gelatin. It should always be rinsed in cold water, then squeezed to remove excess water. After cooking, agar-agar desserts will set at room temperature. They can be reheated without the jelling properties being affected. If a dessert made with agar-agar fails to set, add a tablespoon of arrowroot to a little water and cook for another 5 minutes.

## Aduki Cream Pudding
### (*Makes 8–10 servings*)

This dessert does take some extra time and effort to prepare, but the results are well worth the trouble. It resembles a sinfully rich chocolate mousse, but everything in this pudding is highly nutritious.

1 cup aduki beans
3–3½ cups apple juice
1 bar agar-agar
2½ cups water
1 vanilla bean, split lengthwise
½ teaspoon sea salt
1 tablespoon dry Pero (a grain coffee substitute)
1 cup Puréed Chestnuts
¼ cup Sesame Butter or Almond Butter
3 cups Puréed Rice Cream (recipe follows)
¼ cup roasted whole almonds, optional

Pressure-cook beans in 3 cups apple juice for 45 minutes. For regular cooking, boil beans in 3½ cups apple juice in a covered saucepan for 1½ hours.

While the beans are cooking, wash agar-agar and squeeze out excess water. Tear into small pieces and place in a saucepan with water and vanilla bean. Bring to a boil and skim off any foam that forms. Reduce heat, cover, and simmer for 15 minutes.

Purée beans in a food mill or blender. Remove vanilla bean from agar-agar and beat in salt, puréed beans, dry Pero, puréed chestnuts, and sesame butter. Cook for another 10 minutes, stirring constantly. Beat in puréed rice cream.

Spoon into a large mold or individual dishes and garnish with almonds. Chill for at least 2 hours.

VARIATIONS: Strong grain coffee or mu tea can be used in place of the water in agar-agar preparation. For carob aduki pudding, use ¾ cup carob powder in place of the puréed chestnuts. Chopped dates or figs can be added when cooking agar-agar.


## Puréed Rice Cream
(*Makes 3 cups*)

This is a basic recipe for making plain pudding. It can be made with apple juice instead of water, sweetened with chopped dried fruit, or flavored with vanilla, cinnamon, or other spices. It is used as a base for many recipes in this book.

1½ cups sweet brown rice (or short grain brown rice)
5 cups water
Pinch of salt

Wash rice in cold water and drain. Pan-roast in a dry cast-iron skillet until golden and grains begin to pop. Pour into a pressure cooker, add water and salt, and cook for 40 minutes. Let pot sit undisturbed for 20 minutes after pressure drops. For regular cooking simmer for 1 hour in a covered pan after water comes to a boil.

Purée cooked rice in a food mill. Leftover bran can be used in bread, muffin, or cookie recipes.


## Apple Cream
(*Makes 6 servings*)

4 apples
½ cup apple juice (or orange juice)
3 cups cooked Puréed Rice Cream
4 tablespoons Nut Butter

Slice the apples into thin rounds and simmer in apple juice for 5 minutes. Blend cooked apples with rice and nut butter until smooth and creamy. Serve warm or chilled.

VARIATIONS: Add chopped dried fruit, such as dates or figs. Or try using fresh pears or peaches in place of the apples.

## Apricot Pudding
(*Makes 6 servings*)

This was one of the first pudding recipes I ever tried using only natural foods. It has a somewhat tangy yet sweet taste.

½ pound sun-dried apricots
2½ cups apple juice
¼ teaspoon sea salt
2 cups Puréed Rice Cream
2 tablespoons orange or lemon juice
1 teaspoon grated lemon or orange rind
½ cup roasted and chopped almonds

Cook apricots in juice with salt for 40 minutes in a covered saucepan or pressure-cook for 15 minutes. Purée fruit in a blender or food mill.

Preheat oven to 350° F. Blend fruit, rice, juice, and grated rind. Fold in nuts and spoon into an oiled casserole dish. Bake for 20 minutes.

VARIATIONS: Use ½ cup red wine in place of part of the apple juice. This pudding can also be made with prunes or dried peaches or pears. For a spicy pudding, add ½ teaspoon each cinnamon, cloves, and coriander.

## Barley Parfait
(*Makes 8 servings*)

1 cup barley
6 cups apple juice
½ teaspoon sea salt

1 vanilla bean, split lengthwise
1 bar agar-agar (or 2 teaspoons powdered agar-agar)
1 cup currants or chopped dried fruit
3 pears, chopped
1 cup roasted nuts

Rinse barley and pan-roast in a dry skillet until it changes color. Place barley in a pressure cooker or heavy saucepan with 4 cups juice, salt, and vanilla bean. If pressure cooking, cook with low pressure for 45 minutes. For regular cooking, bring barley to a boil, then cover, reduce flame, and simmer for 1 hour.

While the barley is cooking, wash agar-agar and squeeze out excess water. If using powder, add directly to apple juice. Tear bar into small pieces and place in a saucepan with the remaining apple juice. Bring to a boil and skim off any foam. Add fruit and simmer for 15 minutes, stirring occasionally.

Purée agar-agar mixture in a blender with the nuts. Set aside to cool.

Remove vanilla bean from barley. Purée the barley in a food mill. The leftover bran can be reserved and used for bread or muffin batters. Spoon alternate layers of puréed barley and agar-agar into 8 parfait glasses. Chill for several hours before serving.

VARIATIONS: Puréed Chestnuts or fruit jam can be used in place of the dried fruit.

NOTE: When barley is puréed, bran is a naturally occurring residue.

## Carob Pudding
*(Makes 4 servings)*

1 cup Carob Sauce
1½ cups Puréed Rice Cream, cooked oatmeal, or couscous
¼ cup raisins or chopped dates
2 tablespoons Almond Butter, Cashew Butter, or Sesame Butter
¼ cup crushed nuts

Combine all ingredients except nuts in a blender until creamy. Fold in nuts and spoon into 4 parfait glasses. Chill for at least 1 hour.

VARIATIONS: For Mocha Carob Pudding, add 2 tablespoons dry Pero or a similar grain coffee substitute to blender.

## Carob Frozen Custard
### *(Makes 6 servings)*

1 bar agar-agar
½ cup chopped dates or raisins
3 cups water
3 tablespoons carob powder
1 cup Carob Sauce
¼ cup Nut Butter

Wash agar-agar in cold water. Squeeze out extra water and tear into small pieces. In a saucepan, boil agar-agar with fruit, water, and carob powder for 15 minutes, stirring occasionally. Blend cooked mixture with carob sauce and nut butter. Pour into a freezer tray and freeze just until crystals begin to form around the edge of the tray.

## Bread Pudding
### *(Makes 6–8 generous servings)*

The perfect way to utilize stale bread is to make a fragrant baked pudding.

3 cups cubed bread (whole grain bread)
2 cups mu tea or Grain Coffee
½ cup currants or chopped dried fruit
1 teaspoon ground cinnamon
½ teaspoon sea salt
1 tablespoon grated lemon or orange rind

3 pears or apples, chopped
½ cup chopped nuts
½ cup toasted wheat germ or bran
2 cups Vanilla Sauce or Soy Cream Sauce

Soak bread cubes in mu tea with currants, cinnamon, salt, and lemon rind for several hours or overnight.
Preheat oven to 350° F.
Add apples and nuts to pudding mixture. Oil a casserole and sprinkle with some of the wheat germ. Spoon in pudding and top with remaining wheat germ. Cover dish and bake for 45 minutes. Remove cover and bake for another 10 minutes. Serve hot with chilled vanilla sauce or soy sauce.

## Cherry Couscous Delight
(*Makes about 9 servings*)

Couscous is a very light grain preparation, and this dessert is especially cooling on hot summer days.

2 pints fresh cherries
4 cups liquid (apple juice, water, or mint tea in any
    combination)
½ teaspoon sea salt, divided
1 bar agar-agar
1 cup couscous

Rinse cherries, remove stems, and bring to a boil in a saucepan with liquid and ¼ teaspoon of the sea salt. Cover pan and simmer for 30 minutes. Drain; reserve liquid and force cherries through a sieve or food mill to remove pits.
In a separate pan, bring 3 cups of cooked liquid to a boil. Rinse agar-agar in cold water, squeeze out excess, and tear into small pieces. Drop into boiling liquid. Skim off any foam. Simmer for 15 minutes.
While agar-agar is cooking, boil remaining liquid until it is reduced to 2 cups. Add remaining salt and couscous, simmer for

1 minute, turn off flame, cover immediately, and let sit undisturbed for 15 minutes.

Spread puréed cherries on the bottom of a casserole or mold and cover with couscous. Pour over agar-agar and chill until firm. Cut into large squares.

VARIATIONS: This dish can be made with fresh berries, or 1 pound dried cherries. If you can't find couscous, use 1 cup oat flakes or wheat flakes, and increase cooking time to 30 minutes.

## Chestnut Cream Pudding (*Blancmange*)
(*Makes 6 servings*)

1 stick agar-agar (or 2 teaspoons powdered agar-agar)
4 cups apple juice
1 vanilla bean, split lengthwise
2 tablespoons soybean flour
¾ cup chestnut flour, or 1 cup Puréed Chestnuts
¼ teaspoon salt
¼ cup Sesame Butter or Almond Butter (if salted, eliminate salt in recipe)
¼ cup crushed nuts

Rinse agar-agar in cold water, squeeze out excess water, and tear into pieces. Soak in apple juice for 15 minutes. If using powdered form, eliminate washing and soaking. Pour into a saucepan and bring to a boil. Drop in vanilla bean and simmer for 10 minutes. Slowly add soybean and chestnut flours, stirring constantly to remove lumps. Add salt, lower flame, and cook for another 15 minutes or until thick.

Remove from heat and take out vanilla bean. Blend in sesame butter and beat until smooth. Pour into a mold or 6 individual serving dishes and garnish with crushed nuts. Chill until firm.

VARIATIONS: Add 2 cups cooked and puréed fruit to pudding after cooking. For an attractive parfait, make alternate layers of pudding and Fresh Fruit Glaze in parfait glasses.

# Christmas Rice Pudding

*(A very special extra-rich pudding that makes 12 servings)*

2 cups sweet brown rice (or short grain brown rice)
6 cups strong mu tea or apple juice
1 stick cinnamon
1 vanilla bean, split lengthwise
1 teaspoon sea salt plus ½ teaspoon sea salt
1 cup currants
1 cup monuka (seedless) raisins or chopped dates
1 cup almonds
¾ cup chestnut flour or
   1 cup Puréed Chestnuts
½ cup Sesame Butter

Wash the rice several times in cold water. Soak overnight in 5 cups of the liquid. Pressure-cook the rice with the cinnamon stick, vanilla, and 1 teaspoon salt for 30 minutes. Let rice sit for another 30 minutes before opening pot. For regular cooking, bring to a boil, cover, reduce flame, and simmer for 1 hour.

Preheat oven to 350° F.

While the rice is cooking, simmer the currants and raisins in a saucepan with 1 cup liquid and ½ teaspoon sea salt for 10 minutes. Roast the almonds in the oven for 10–15 minutes, or until lightly roasted.

Strain the cooked fruit; pour cooking liquid into a bowl and beat in chestnut flour and sesame butter. Purée cooked rice in a food mill and add to the chestnut mixture. Beat in raisins and almonds (save a few for garnish). Spoon mixture into an oiled 2-quart casserole and bake for 40 minutes.

This pudding is almost as dense as a bread and may be served by cutting it into ½-inch thick slices. It is especially good chilled and will keep for several days in the refrigerator.

VARIATIONS: Dried figs or apricots can be used in place of the raisins. Lemon or orange juice and grated rind can be used in place of the cinnamon. For a chocolate flavor, use ¾ cup carob powder in place of the chestnut flour. Pecans may be used in place of the almonds. Serve with Soy Cream Sauce or Carob Sauce, or try a Fresh Fruit Glaze.

## Coffee Mousse
*(Makes 6–8 servings)*

2 bars agar-agar
2 cups apple juice
2 cups strong grain or dandelion coffee
1 vanilla bean, split lengthwise
A dash of salt
½ cup Sesame Butter or Almond Butter

Rinse agar-agar in cold water. Squeeze out excess water. Tear agar-agar into small pieces and soak in liquids for 20 minutes. Bring to a boil in a saucepan with vanilla bean and salt and simmer uncovered for 20 minutes, stirring occasionally.* Remove bean.

Pour gelatin into a blender, add sesame butter, and blend until creamy. Pour into a dessert mold and chill until firm or freeze until crystals begin to form around the edges.

VARIATIONS: Add ¼ cup crushed nuts to gelatin. For a mocha-flavored gelatin, add 2–3 tablespoons carob powder during last 5 minutes of cooking. Two heaping tablespoons Pero and 2 cups water can be used in place of grain coffee or dandelion coffee.

---

* As with all agar-agar desserts, skim to remove any foam that forms. The foam results from slight impurities in the seaweed gelatin.

## Couscous Pudding
*(Makes 6–8 servings)*

3 cups apple (or any other fruit) juice
1 cup raw couscous
½ cup chopped dried fruit
½ cup chopped walnuts or almonds
½ teaspoon sea salt
4 tablespoons Nut Butter

Bring fruit juice to a boil in a 2-quart saucepan. Add remaining ingredients, bring to a boil again, and simmer for 2 minutes, stirring constantly. Cover and turn off heat. Let sit undisturbed for 15 minutes.

Serve either warm or spoon into serving dishes and chill.

VARIATIONS: Serve with Soy Cream Sauce or Fresh Fruit Glaze.

## Couscous Blueberry Surprise
*(Makes 9 servings)*

1 pint fresh blueberries
1 cup fruit juice
1 tablespoon lemon juice
2 tablespoons arrowroot flour starch
4 cups cooked Couscous Pudding

Preheat oven to 375° F.

Rinse blueberries in cold water. Bring blueberries and fruit juice and lemon juice to a boil in a saucepan. Remove some of the liquid and use to dissolve the starch. Add starch to blueberries, stirring constantly. Remove from heat when thick. Spread the bottom of a cake pan with a layer of couscous. Pour over blueberries, then remaining couscous and cover with blueberries. Bake in oven for 25 minutes.

## Eggless Apple Custard
(*Makes about 6 servings*)

3 cups apple juice
1 vanilla bean, split lengthwise
¼ teaspoon sea salt
¼ cup Sesame Butter
3 apples, cored and thinly sliced
3 tablespoons arrowroot flour starch
1 cup cold water
¼ cup slivered almonds

Place apple juice and vanilla bean in a 2-quart saucepan with sea salt. Cover and simmer for 15 minutes. Remove vanilla bean. Dilute sesame butter with a small amount of hot apple juice and add to pan. Bring mixture to a boil and add apple slices.

Dilute arrowroot starch with 1 cup cold water; add to custard and bring to a boil, stirring constantly. Lower flame and simmer for a few minutes more.

Pour custard into 6 tall parfait glasses or soufflé cups and garnish with almonds. Chill for several hours before serving.


## Grain Pudding
(*Makes 6 servings*)

1 cup whole-wheat flour or Wheatena
4 cups liquid (water, grain coffee, or mu tea)
½ cup currants, chopped dates, or figs
1 vanilla bean, split lengthwise
1 teaspoon sea salt
½ cup crushed nuts (or sunflower seed meal or sesame seeds, crushed)
1 teaspoon cinnamon

Heat a dry cast-iron skillet. Pour in flour and stir constantly until flour is nut brown and fragrant. Set pan aside to cool.

In a saucepan, bring liquid, fruit, vanilla bean, and sea salt to a boil. Cover and simmer for 15 minutes. Remove vanilla bean and drain fruit, reserving liquid.

Let liquid cool for at least 5 minutes. Add liquid to roasted flour gradually. When all liquid is added, return skillet to heat and cook uncovered for 30 minutes. Stir occasionally to prevent burning.

Add fruit and nuts and cover pan. Cook for another 30 minutes, stirring every now and then. Add cinnamon during last 5 minutes of cooking. It helps to place an asbestos pad under pan. Pour pudding into a ceramic or glass bowl that has been rinsed in cold water. Chill for several hours.

## Indian Corn Pudding
(*Makes 6 servings*)

⅔ cup white corn meal

3 cups apple juice

½ cup currants or chopped dried fruit

2 apples, grated

½ cup chopped nuts

4 tablespoons soybean flour

2 tablespoons corn or sesame oil plus extra oil for pan

½ teaspoon sea salt

1 teaspoon cinnamon

1 egg

Dry-roast the corn meal in a cast-iron skillet for 10 minutes until it darkens slightly. Preheat oven to 350° F.

Bring apple juice to a boil and add currants. Cover and simmer for 15 minutes. Pour corn meal into a mixing bowl and scald with hot apple juice. Stir quickly to prevent lumping. Let cool for a few minutes before beating in other ingredients.

Bake for 1 hour in an oiled casserole. Serve either hot or cold.

## Lemon Cream Custard
*(Makes 6 servings)*

6 tablespoons sweet rice flour
4 tablespoons corn oil
2 tablespoons soybean flour
4 cups apple juice
½ teaspoon sea salt
1 lemon
1 teaspoon vanilla extract

In a heavy saucepan, pan-roast the rice flour in oil for a few minutes. Let cool and mix in soy flour. Stir in apple juice gradually, until mixture is free of lumps.

Return to heat and bring to a boil over a medium flame. Stir occasionally. Add sea salt and simmer over a low flame for 20 minutes.

Grate lemon rind and add to custard. Squeeze out 1 tablespoon lemon juice and add to pan. Cook for 5 minutes, add vanilla extract, and stir well. Remove pan from heat. Let cool and spoon into dessert glasses.

## Steamed Grain Pudding
*(Makes 6–8 servings)*

This recipe works well with cooked leftover brown rice, wheat berries, whole oats, or millet.

3 tablespoons soybean flour
1 cup apple juice
1½ cups water
½ teaspoon sea salt
1 vanilla bean, split lengthwise
3 tablespoons Sesame Butter
1 cup currants or chopped dates

2½ cups cooked grain, any cereal
½ cup chopped walnuts
1 tablespoon grated tangerine or orange rind
½ teaspoon nutmeg

Preheat oven to 350° F.

In a saucepan, combine soybean flour, apple juice, water, and sea salt. Bring to a boil, add vanilla bean, and lower heat. Cover pan and simmer for 15 minutes.

Remove vanilla bean and beat in sesame butter. Mix in other ingredients. Use a wooden spoon to separate grains if cereal is somewhat solidified.

Transfer pudding mixture to an oiled casserole, cover, and bake for 45 minutes. Remove cover and bake for another 10 minutes.

This dessert tastes best when served still warm.

## Steamed Bran Pudding

(*Makes 6–8 servings*)

3 cups wheat bran or rice bran
4 cups grain coffee or apple juice
½ teaspoon sea salt
1 cup currants
2 tablespoons soybean flour or chestnut flour
2 tablespoons arrowroot flour starch
1 cup cooked grain (any cereal)
⅓ cup crushed nuts
1 teaspoon cinnamon
¼ teaspoon nutmeg
Soy Cream Sauce or Carob Sauce, optional

Preheat oven to 350° F.

Toast the bran in a dry cast-iron skillet, stirring constantly to prevent burning, for about 5 minutes. Pour into a mixing bowl.

In a saucepan bring liquid, salt, and currants to a boil and simmer for 10 minutes. Pour hot liquid and currants over the bran and mix well. Beat in flours, cooked grain, nuts, and spices.

Pour pudding into an oiled 2-quart casserole and cover. Bake for 2 hours; remove cover during the last 30 minutes of baking. Serve with either soy cream or carob sauce if desired.

## *Strawberry Mousse*
*(Makes 8 servings)*

2 pints fresh strawberries
¼ teaspoon sea salt
1 bar agar-agar (or 2 teaspoons powder*)
1 vanilla bean, split lengthwise
2 cups apple juice
1 cup Puréed Rice Cream, or cooked oatmeal
½ cup Sesame Butter or Almond Butter

Slice strawberries, reserving a couple for garnish, and place on a large platter. Sprinkle with salt and set aside.

Rinse agar-agar in cold water, squeeze out excess liquid, and tear into several pieces. Place in a saucepan with vanilla bean and apple juice and simmer for 15 minutes, stirring occasionally. Turn off flame and add strawberries. The heat will cause them to change to a bright pink, but they should not be cooked. Remove vanilla bean.

In a blender beat together rice cream, sesame butter, and agar-agar mixture. Pour into 8 individual glasses or a gelatin mold and chill until firm. Garnish with whole strawberries. Mousse may also be set in freezer until crystals begin to form around the edges.

VARIATIONS: Raspberries or loganberries may be used in place of strawberries.

---

* If you are using powdered agar-agar, add directly to liquid and eliminate washing.

## Whipped Prune Mousse
*(Makes 8 ½-cup servings)*

This is a very simple, smooth-textured dessert that goes well anytime of the year. It has the consistency of a dessert made with fresh cream.

2 bars agar-agar
6 cups cold water
1 pound sun-dried prunes
1 teaspoon vanilla extract
1 cup sunflower seeds

Wash the bars of agar-agar and break into small pieces. Place in a saucepan with 2 cups water and let soak for 30 minutes. While the agar-agar is soaking, place the prunes and remaining water in a pressure cooker or heavy saucepan and cook until the prunes are very soft. If pressure cooking, cook for only 10 minutes. For regular cooking, allow at least 40 minutes. Let cool and remove pits.

Bring the agar-agar to a boil and simmer for 15 minutes over a low heat. Skim surface to remove any film. Drain cooking liquid from prunes and add to agar-agar mixture and cook for another 5 minutes. Add vanilla extract.

In a separate pan, dry-roast the sunflower seeds until they are lightly roasted. Pour about ⅓ of the agar-agar mixture into a blender and add the sunflower seeds. Blend until the seeds are homogenized with the pudding. Gradually add remaining liquid. Pour off half of the pudding into a bowl and add the pitted prunes to the remaining liquid in the blender. Blend again until the prunes are completely puréed.

Either pour prune mixture over the agar-agar base in a large mold, or spoon separate layers of the 2 puddings into parfait glasses. Chill for 2 hours.

# Chapter 12. *Simple Fruit and Vegetable Desserts*

The recipes found in this chapter are for simple, light desserts that satisfy a desire for something sweet but are relatively low in calories and not very rich. They are perfect desserts for lunchtime, or they complement a hearty dinner menu.

Certain vegetables, such as carrots, pumpkin, and squash, combine very well with fruit and lend a delightful color as well as taste to dessert preparations.

## *Apples in Snow*
### (*Makes 6 servings*)

This recipe is sort of a reverse sundae—hot baked apples set in a bed of creamy cold sauce. It's visually appealing as well as delicious and makes a perfect late fall or winter dessert.

6 large apples
1 teaspoon sea salt
½ cup raisins or 6 dates, pitted
⅓ cup apple juice
3 cups Vanilla Sauce, well chilled

Preheat oven to 350° F.

Core apples but do not peel. Rub a small amount of salt into each hollow and fill with raisins or dates. Place apples in a baking dish and add juice. Cover dish and bake for 50 minutes.

To serve, place a generous dollop of vanilla sauce in a dessert dish and set hot apple on top. Sauce may be peaked to resemble a snowdrift.

VARIATIONS: Use whole baked pears in place of apples. Cinnamon, nutmeg, or slivered almonds can be used as a garnish.

## Baked Pears
### (*Makes 6 servings*)

A simple and attractive dessert. For extra richness, serve with Vanilla Sauce.

6 large pears
¼ cup sea salt
1 cup apple or orange juice
1 heaping tablespoon arrowroot flour starch
¼ teaspoon nutmeg
¼ teaspoon ground ginger

Preheat oven to 350° F.

Wash pears thoroughly in cold water and cut in half lengthwise. Place pears in a baking dish and sprinkle with salt. Pour in juice and cover pan. Bake for 30 minutes.

Remove cover and drain off cooking liquid. Mix reserved liquid with arrowroot starch. Return sauce to pan and sprinkle pears with nutmeg and ginger. Cover pan and bake for another 15–20 minutes, basting fruit occasionally with glaze.

## Carrot Pudding
(*Makes 6 servings*)

For a change of pace, it's nice to serve a vegetable dessert. Sautéing the carrots before steaming makes them much sweeter.

2 pounds fresh carrots
1 tablespoon sesame oil
2 cups liquid (herbal tea or fruit juice)
2 tablespoons arrowroot flour starch
½ cup Puréed Chestnuts
½ teaspoon sea salt
½ teaspoon cinnamon

Slice carrots diagonally into thin rounds. Heat oil in a skillet and sauté carrots over a high flame for 10 minutes. Add 1 cup liquid, cover pan, and simmer for 30 minutes, or pressure-cook for 10 minutes.

Drain carrots, reserving cooking liquid, and purée in a food mill. Return liquid to pan, stir in arrowroot until dissolved, then add remaining liquid, puréed carrots, chestnuts, salt, and spice. Simmer for 10 minutes or until very thick. Pudding may also be poured into a casserole and baked for 20 minutes at 375° F.

VARIATIONS: Any variety of fall squash, such as buttercup, butternut, or pumpkin, may be used in place of the carrots. For a richer pudding, blend in 2–4 tablespoons Almond or Sesame Butter and garnish with crushed nuts and a dash of nutmeg.

## Fresh Fruit Gelatin
(*Makes 4 servings*)

1 bar agar-agar
2½ cups apple juice
1 pint crushed fresh fruit (berries, peaches, etc.)
A pinch of salt

Rinse agar-agar and squeeze out excess liquid. Tear into small pieces and soak in apple juice for 20 minutes. Bring to a boil in a heavy saucepan and simmer for 20 minutes, stirring occasionally. Add fruit and salt and simmer for a few more minutes. Remove from heat and pour into a mold or dessert glasses. Chill until firm.

VARIATIONS: Cubes of cantaloupe or muskmelon are especially good in summer in place of the crushed fruit. Combine gelatin in a blender with ¼ cup Nut Butter after it has set. Pour into a mold and chill again until firm.

NOTE: Agar-agar desserts will set at room temperature but turn out best when served chilled. If a dessert made with agar-agar fails to set, too much liquid may have been used in preparation. A loose gelatin can be quickly restored by reheating. Add 1 tablespoon of arrowroot flour starch (more or less, depending upon thickness of gelatin) and cook for a few minutes. Chill and serve.

## Glazed Apples
(*Makes 4 servings*)

4–5 large tart red apples
2½ cups apple or orange juice
½ teaspoon cinnamon
¼ teaspoon sea salt
1 tablespoon dry Pero (grain coffee substitute)
1 heaping tablespoon arrowroot flour starch or kuzu

Wash apples thoroughly. Cut into thin rounds. Bring 2 cups of the juice to a boil in a deep saucepan or skillet. Add cinnamon and salt and then boil several apple rings at a time for 3–5 minutes. Remove cooked apples with a slotted spoon and repeat process until all fruit is cooked.

Dilute Pero and arrowroot with remaining juice. Mix well and add to cooking liquid. Simmer, stirring constantly until mixture becomes thick. Pour glaze over apples and serve warm or chilled. Makes a delightful accompaniment to cookies.

VARIATIONS: Other firm fresh fruit, such as peaches, pears, or nectarines, can be used in place of apples. Red wine can be used in place of part of the liquid. Currants or raisins can be added during the cooking.

## Pumpkin Chestnut Compote
(*Makes 2 quarts*)

This dessert is not terribly sweet but is completely satisfying (at least to me and about a dozen unknowing guinea pigs I conned into trying it). It may be served warm or cold and combines well with cookies or a light creamy pudding.

1 medium-size pumpkin (about 5–6 pounds)
1 cup strong mu tea or apple cider
½ teaspoon sea salt
1 pound fresh or dried chestnuts
8 tart red apples, cored and chopped with skins left on
1 teaspoon cinnamon
½ teaspoon ground ginger
¼ teaspoon nutmeg
½ cup chopped roasted almonds

Scrub pumpkin carefully and cut in half. Remove seeds and membrane. Cut flesh into 1-inch cubes and place in a large pot with mu tea and salt. Bring liquid to a boil over a high flame, then cover pan, lower flame, and steam for 40 minutes, or until pumpkin is easily pierced with a wooden skewer or fork.

If you are using fresh chestnuts, make a gash in the outer skin and boil chestnuts in 6 cups water for 15 minutes. Drain and rinse in cold water. Chestnuts may also be baked in a covered pan with about 1 cup water in a 375° F. oven for the same amount of time. If you are using dried chestnuts, see directions for preparation in recipe for making Chestnut Purée.

Add apples, chestnuts, and spices and simmer uncovered for at least 45 minutes. The longer this mixture cooks, the sweeter and thicker it becomes. Don't be surprised if there is a large amount of water—pumpkin is very high in water and loses most of its volume in cooking.

Add nuts just before serving.

VARIATIONS: For a creamy compote, add ½ cup Nut Butter during the last 5 minutes of cooking. Compote can also be baked in a slow oven for several hours.

## Pumpkin Pudding or Pie Filling
(*Makes 6–8 servings*)

1 medium-size pumpkin (about 5–6 pounds) or fall squash
1 tablespoon sesame oil
½ teaspoon sea salt
2 cups apple juice
¾ cup chestnut flour or 1 cup Puréed Chestnuts
2 tablespoons arrowroot flour starch
¼ cup Nut Butter or Peanut Butter
½ teaspoon each cinnamon, fresh grated ginger, ground cloves
¼ teaspoon nutmeg, optional

Scrub the pumpkin thoroughly. With a heavy knife, cut the pumpkin in half and scoop out the seeds,* then quarter and cut into sections following the veins as a guide. Cut crosswise into 1-inch cubes.

Heat oil in a large, heavy skillet or pot and sauté the cubes over a high flame for 10 minutes. Add salt and juice. Bring to a

* The seeds are very good to eat. Simply wash well in cold water, spread on a cookie sheet, and bake in a 200° F. oven for 1–2 hours.

boil, then cover, lower flame, and let steam for 45 minutes, or until flesh is easily pierced with a fork. If pressure cooking, cook for 15 minutes once the pressure goes up. Drain out liquid and reserve; mash the pulp or put through a food mill. Return cooking liquid to pan and beat in other ingredients with a whisk. Add puréed pumpkin and cook until thick, stirring occasionally.

This pudding can be either poured into a mold and chilled, or baked in an oiled casserole in a 325° F. oven for 30 minutes. For pumpkin pie, pour into a 10-minute baked piecrust and bake for another 25 minutes.

## Squash Compote
*(Makes 6–8 servings)*

1 tablespoon vegetable oil
4 pounds butternut, buttercup, or other fall squash, cubed
2 pounds tart red apples, cored and chopped
Fruit juice (orange or apple)
1 tablespoon lemon juice, 1 teaspoon grated rind
⅔ cup chopped almonds
½ teaspoon sea salt
½ teaspoon cinnamon
Nutmeg, optional

Heat oil in a large heavy skillet or pot. Sauté squash over a high flame for 5 minutes, add apples, and sauté for another 5 minutes. Add remaining ingredients to pan, cover, and steam for 30–40 minutes, adding a little fruit juice if compote looks too dry. Serve warm or cold.

VARIATIONS: Use fresh ginger juice in place of the lemon. Grate a 2-inch piece of peeled gingerroot, squeeze out juice, and discard stringy pulp. Chopped dates, figs, dried apricots, or currants can be added. The possibilities for experimenting with different fruits and spices are endless.

## Watermelon Compote
### (*Makes 12–15 servings*)

This is a sumptuous summer festival of flavors, perfect to serve for large parties. And don't be afraid to cook the watermelon! It makes a wonderful ruby-colored sauce.

1 large watermelon (about 20 pounds)
½ teaspoon sea salt
4 tablespoons arrowroot flour starch
2 pints fresh strawberries
2 lemons
2 oranges
4 ripe peaches
Watercress or mint leaves for garnish

Cut watermelon in half crosswise. Scoop out pulp and deseed. Save half of the pulp and purée the rest in a blender. Reserve ½ cup of the puréed fruit and place remaining puréed fruit in a large pot. Bring to a boil and let cook, uncovered, with salt for 1 hour. This concentrates the juice and makes a sweeter syrup.

Dilute arrowroot flour in reserved liquid. Add to cooked syrup and simmer for another 5 minutes.

While syrup is cooking, wash and slice strawberries. Slice citrus fruit into very thin rounds, peaches into thin crescents. Add fruit to hot syrup and simmer for 1 minute. Remove from heat and let cool for at least 15 minutes before adding reserved watermelon pulp. Pour compote into watermelon shells and chill. If your refrigerator isn't big enough to hold watermelon shells, chill compote in a large bowl or two and transfer to shells just before serving. Garnish with fresh watercress or mint leaves.

## Watermelon Gelatin
(*Makes 6–8 servings*)

7 pounds watermelon (or enough to make 1 quart liquid plus
   1½ cups cubed fruit)
1 cup strong mint tea
¼ teaspoon sea salt
2 bars agar-agar
1 teaspoon lemon juice
Fresh whole strawberries or cherries for garnish

Remove the seeds from the watermelon. Reserve about 1½
cups cubed fruit, then place the remaining amount in a blender to
liquify, or force through a food mill sieve, or fine strainer.

Place the juice in a 2-quart saucepan with the mint tea and salt
and bring to a boil. Rinse agar-agar in cold water and squeeze out
excess water. Tear into small pieces and add to watermelon mixture. Simmer uncovered for 20 minutes, skimming off any foam
that forms. Stir occasionally to prevent sticking.

Add lemon juice and simmer for another 5 minutes. Pour agar-
agar into a mold. Let set at room temperature for about 30
minutes. Add fruit cubes and refrigerate until firm. Garnish with
strawberries or cherries and serve.

VARIATION: To make watermelon sherbet, proceed as above
but eliminate cubed fruit and add 1 more cup watermelon juice
instead. Pour into ice-cube trays and freeze until crystals begin
to form and serve.

# Chapter 13. *A Potpourri of Fruit & Nut Butters, Toppings, Fillings, Glazes, and Sauces*

This chapter is devoted to those little extras that lend a very special touch to desserts. Some of them can stand alone as simple desserts, but when combined with other desserts, they create minor culinary masterpieces.

Included are sauces and spreads that can be used as toppings or swirled into cake, muffin, or cookie batters; fillings that can be used to stuff pastries or crêpes, or simply enjoyed over a slice of fresh baked bread or crackers.

All have been designed for the modern kitchen, and although some of the recipes do involve long cooking processes, they are not elaborate or complicated.

## *Amasake*

Amasake is a grain-based fermented dish that is used as a base for sweet desserts. Koji rice, available in Oriental and natural food stores, is used as a starter for the fermentation process. It is treated with a special yeast culture, *Aspergillus oryzae,* which converts the starch found in rice into a simpler sugar. However, the sugar is not refined, as in the case of cane sugar, and it is not as concentrated as honey, maple syrup, molasses, or sorghum.

2 cups sweet brown rice (or sweet white rice)
3½ cups water
¼ cup koji soaked in ½ cup water
¼ teaspoon sea salt

Ideally, both the rice and koji should be soaked overnight. If not, at least soak for several hours before cooking. Pressure-cook rice in water for 45 minutes, or simmer in a covered saucepan for 1 hour. Transfer rice to a ceramic or glass container and let cool until it is warm (about 80° F.). Add soaked koji and gently mix.

Cover container and let sit in a warm place for at least 12 hours, stirring occasionally to allow for uniform fermentation. Amasake may be left to ferment for up to 48 hours, but then it will resemble a sweet rice wine.

Amasake may be used in this form for puddings, cakes, etc. If it is not to be used immediately, add salt and simmer for a few minutes over a low heat to stop fermentation.

For Amasake Syrup: Purée fermented amasake in a food mill to remove bran. Boil purée in a large, heavy saucepan (to prevent splattering) until thick, stirring occasionally. This syrup may then be used as a topping for crêpes or other desserts. It will keep, refrigerated, for about 2 weeks. Leftover bran is good in bread or muffin batters.

## Carob Sauce
(*Makes about 3 cups*)

Carob closely resembles chocolate in appearance, has a natural sweet taste (unlike chocolate, which is naturally bitter), and is low in fat as well as high in protein. However, because it has a somewhat chalky taste when used alone, you may find it better to use this sauce in dessert preparations rather than plain as a sweetening agent.

8 tablespoons dry carob powder
3 cups water
1 vanilla bean, split lengthwise
¼ teaspoon sea salt
2 tablespoons soybean flour
½ cup currants, raisins, or chopped dates
1 heaping tablespoon arrowroot flour starch
1 heaping tablespoon Pero (a grain coffee substitute)

Dissolve carob in water and bring to a boil in a saucepan. Drop in vanilla bean and salt and cover pan, simmer for 15 minutes. Remove vanilla bean and beat in soy flour with a whisk or egg beater. Add fruit. Cover and simmer for another 15 minutes. Remove a small amount of liquid and use to dissolve arrowroot.

Add dissolved arrowroot and Pero. Stir constantly until thick. Sauce will thicken in a few minutes. Pour into a blender and liquefy. Use sauce over puddings, cakes, or add to muffin or cookie batters for a chocolate taste.

VARIATIONS: For a fudgie frosting, add 2–4 tablespoons Sesame Butter or Almond Butter, 2 tablespoons dry carob, and blend again.

## Cranberry Applesauce
(*Makes about 7 cups*)

1 pound fresh cranberries
1 cup apple cider
⅛ teaspoon sea salt
3 pounds small red apples, cored and chopped
½ teaspoon cinnamon
½ cup currants
1 tablespoon lemon juice, optional
Grated lemon or orange rind

Rinse cranberries in cold water and sort out spoiled fruit. Bring apple cider to a boil in a heavy, deep saucepan or pressure cooker and add salt and cranberries. Boil until cranberries begin to pop. Add remaining ingredients and cover. Simmer for another 20 minutes.* Purée sauce if desired. Serve either warm or chilled. This sauce goes wonderfully with sweet breads, cookies, and muffins.

VARIATIONS: To make a cranberry glaze, dilute 1 heaping tablespoon arrowroot flour starch in a small amount of apple cider and add to sauce during the last 5 minutes of cooking. Ginger juice can be used in place of lemon juice, or try another dried fruit, such as figs or apricots, in place of the currants.

* If pressure cooking, reduce cooking time to 10 minutes.

## Dried Fruit Purée or Jam
(*Makes about 1 quart*)

1 pound dried apricots, figs, currants, peaches, or prunes
2 cups strong mu tea or mint tea
1 cup apple cider
¼ teaspoon sea salt
1 bar agar-agar, washed and soaked in 1 cup apple juice for
  30 minutes
Grated lemon or orange rind
Cinnamon, optional

The night before, soak dried fruit in tea and cider. Add salt
and pressure-cook for 20 minutes or simmer in a covered saucepan
for 1 hour.

Purée fruit in a blender or food mill. Return to pot, add agar-
agar, rind, and cinnamon, and simmer uncovered for 20 minutes,
stirring occasionally to prevent sticking.

Use purée as a spread, pie filling, or topping for muffins, cakes,
or breads. It can be stored in glass jars and kept refrigerated for a
week.

VARIATIONS: A combination of dried fruit makes an interesting
flavor. Use sweeter fruits, such as currants or raisins, with a more
tart one, such as apricots. Arrowroot flour starch can be used in
place of agar-agar (use about 2 tablespoons and reduce cooking
time to 10 minutes).

## Fruit Syrup and Jelly
*(Makes about 1 quart)*

This syrup may be used as a sweetening agent in recipes calling for fruit juice, or thickened to use as a topping for pancakes, waffles, crêpes, or puddings. It will keep without spoiling for several weeks when stored in the refrigerator.

2 pounds currants, raisins, figs, or pitted prunes
10 cups water or mu tea
½ teaspoon sea salt

Bring currants and water to a boil in a large, heavy saucepan. Lower flame, add salt, and cover pan. Simmer for 2 hours.

Drain syrup, reserving liquid. Leftover fruit pulp may be used in cake or cookie batter. Return liquid to pan and boil down to desired sweetness.

VARIATIONS: For thicker syrup, dissolve 2 tablespoons arrowroot flour starch in a small amount of syrup, return to pan, and simmer for a few minutes, or until syrup is clear and thick. Thickened syrup can be used as a fruit jelly.

## Fresh Fruit Glaze
*(Makes about 1 quart)*

1 cup apple cider
4 cups crushed fresh fruit (peaches, apricots, nectarines, plums, etc.)
¼ teaspoon sea salt
2 tablespoons arrowroot flour starch or kuzu
¼ cup strong mint tea

Bring cider to a boil in a heavy saucepan. Add fruit and salt and bring to a boil again. Cover pan and simmer for 15 minutes.

Dilute arrowroot in tea. Add immediately to cooked fruit and cook for another 5 minutes or until thick.

VARIATIONS: Use orange juice in place of cider. Fresh grated lemon or orange rind or gingerroot adds extra zip. Chopped dried fruit, crushed nuts, or seeds can be added. Serve chilled as a simple dessert, or use as a topping for puddings, muffins, breads, or cake.

## Puréed Chestnuts

French cuisine has long been familiar with chestnuts. They have such a lovely sweet flavor and change so many other foods that it's a shame not to try using them occasionally. They are extremely low in fat and have only ⅓ as many calories as other nuts.

1½ pounds fresh chestnuts or
  2 cups dried chestnuts
Water

If you are using fresh chestnuts, wash them and cut a slit in the skin. Bake in a preheated 350° F. oven for 30 minutes, or until chestnuts are soft. Test for softness by removing a chestnut and peeling. Inside meat should be easily pierced with a toothpick. If chestnuts are baked too long, they will become very hard. However, all is not lost, for these baked nuggets are delicious and can be used in another dish if they are gently steamed for a few minutes—but they can't be used in a purée unless the meat is very soft.

Let chestnuts cool and then peel. Mash slightly, then purée in a blender with a small amount of water until creamy.

If you are using dried chestnuts, soak overnight or for several hours in cold water. Drain and bring to a boil or pressure-cook in enough water to cover. Drain again and purée as above.

Fresh chestnuts are easy to obtain in the fall. Most of them are imported because American chestnuts are becoming almost extinct. The fried chestnuts can be found year round in Oriental markets, Italian grocery stores, or health food stores.

This purée can be used in many different recipes or served as a dessert with a garnish of chopped nuts.


## *Sesame Glaze*
### (*Makes about 1 pint*)

This is a great emergency glaze—it takes only about 10 minutes to make and is very easy to prepare.

2 cups apple juice
1 vanilla bean
4 tablespoons Sesame Butter
1 heaping tablespoon arrowroot flour starch or kuzu

Simmer apple juice and vanilla bean in a covered saucepan for 10 minutes. Remove vanilla bean and ¼ cup juice. Beat sesame butter in with a whisk or egg beater. Return to heat and simmer for 5 minutes. Dilute arrowroot in reserved liquid and stir into glaze. Remove from heat as soon as glaze is thick. Use as a topping for cakes, cookies, or fruit desserts.

VARIATIONS: Nut butters can be used in place of sesame butter. Grated lemon or orange rind can be added to spike the taste. For orange glaze, use orange juice in place of apple juice. Or try cherry juice for a delightful pink-colored glaze.

## Soy Cream Sauce
### (*Makes about 1 pint*)

This is a delightfully deceiving sauce—it is rich-tasting but light and economical as well. It goes well over crêpes, pastries, or plain fruit desserts.

2 tablespoons soybean flour
2¼ cups apple juice
1 vanilla bean, split lengthwise
1 lemon
1 heaping tablespoon arrowroot flour starch
2 tablespoons corn germ oil
Dash of salt

Dissolve soybean flour in 2 cups apple juice in a saucepan. Bring to a boil, add vanilla bean, and stir constantly until thick. This should be done over an asbestos pad or double boiler because soybean flour burns easily.

After about 5 minutes, cut lemon in half and squeeze about 1 tablespoon of juice into arrowroot. Add remaining apple juice and mix into a paste. Stir arrowroot mixture into sauce and cook for another 5 minutes, stirring constantly.

Remove from stove and let cool for a few minutes. Remove vanilla bean and grate a teaspoon of lemon rind into sauce. Heat oil in a separate pan to remove raw taste.

Pour sauce into a blender or deep bowl and beat until foamy. Add salt and slowly add the oil, a drop at a time, and continue beating until sauce is smooth.

Serve as a sauce over a warm dessert, or chill in a freezer and serve as a custard over cooked fruit, cookies, etc.

VARIATIONS: For orange sauce, use orange juice in place of apple juice. Makes a delicious orange sherbet when frozen until slushy.

## Super Granola
(*Makes about 16 cups*)

Granola is a great snack food as well as a handy topping for just about any dessert. Store in glass containers.

5 cups oat flakes
5 cups wheat flakes
1 cup sesame seeds
½ cup flax seeds
1 cup sunflower seeds
1 cup wheat germ
1 cup slivered almonds or chopped walnuts or cashews

SYRUP:

1 cup pure barley malt extract, Amasake, or Fruit Syrup
1½ cups fruit juice
1 tablespoon sea salt
1 tablespoon vanilla extract and/or
   1 tablespoon almond extract
½ cup safflower oil
1–2 cups raisins, chopped dates, or figs, optional

Dry-roast flakes, a cup at a time, in a large cast-iron skillet. Stir constantly to prevent burning and remove flakes when they are lightly toasted. Pour flakes into a large bowl.

Rinse sesame seeds and dry-roast as for the flakes. Pour roasted seeds into bowl with flakes. Add remaining seeds, wheat germ, and nuts and mix thoroughly.

Preheat oven to 300° F.

In a saucepan combine barley malt, fruit juice, sea salt, and extracts. Bring to a boil and simmer for a few minutes, stirring constantly. Remove from heat and stir in oil. Pour syrup over granola mixture and mix well, tossing the ingredients as if you were making a tossed salad, until everything is well coated.

Spread several cups of the mixture at a time onto cookie sheets and bake for about 45 minutes, stirring occasionally with a wooden spoon or spatula to prevent burning. When all of granola is baked, mix in fruit, let mixture cool, and store in airtight glass containers.

VARIATIONS: Absolutely endless. For cinnamon-flavored granola, add 1–2 tablespoons ground cinnamon. For chocolate-flavored granola, add ½ cup carob powder and ¼ cup more fruit juice to syrup. For orange-flavored granola, use 2 tablespoons orange extract in place of vanilla and add 2 tablespoons finely grated orange rind.

Chopped dried apples, apricots, peaches, or prunes can be used in place of raisins.

## *Tangy Applesauce*
(*Makes 1–2 quarts*)

5–10 pounds tart red apples (wild apples taste best)
1 cup mint or mu tea
Juice and grated rind of 1 small lemon
½ teaspoon sea salt
1–2 cinnamon sticks

Wash the apples thoroughly. Slice into eighths and place in a heavy saucepan or pressure cooker with remaining ingredients. Cook for 30 minutes, stirring occasionally to prevent burning. If pressure cooking, bring up pressure and cook for 15 minutes.

Remove cinnamon sticks and force pulp through a food mill or sieve to remove skins and seeds. The secret of this method is cooking apples with the skins to give the sauce a rich rosy color.

VARIATIONS: For a sweeter sauce, add 1 cup currants or raisins to cooked applesauce and simmer for another 15 minutes in a covered pan. Arrowroot flour starch dissolved in a little apple cider can be used to thicken sauce if desired.

## Apple Butter

Cook puréed applesauce down in a heavy saucepan or cast-iron pot until dark and volume is reduced by ⅔. Stir occasionally to prevent burning. This procedure takes hours—so plan to be near the stove. If you like your apple butter on the spicy side, add ground cloves, allspice, or ginger.

## Vanilla Sauce
### (*Makes about 3 cups*)

This sauce is especially good with baked fruit or plain pastries. It enhances just about any dish and may also be served alone as a pudding.

½ cup Sesame Butter
½ cup sweet rice flour
⅛ teaspoon sea salt
1 vanilla bean, split lengthwise, or 1 teaspoon pure vanilla
    extract
3 cups apple juice

Pour oil off the top of the sesame butter and pour into a saucepan. If there is no excess oil, use 2 tablespoons sesame oil. Heat oil over a low flame and add flour. Sauté for a few minutes and remove from heat.

Add remaining ingredients and beat with a whisk to eliminate lumps. (If you are using vanilla extract, don't add until last few minutes of cooking.) Bring sauce to a boil over a medium heat, lower flame, and simmer uncovered for 30 minutes, stirring occasionally.

Sauce is ready to use warm, or it may be chilled and whipped for a lighter consistency.

VARIATIONS: For carob vanilla sauce, use ¼ cup carob powder in place of ¼ cup rice flour. Almond extract may be used in place of vanilla for almond sauce. Grated lemon or orange rind is also pleasant.

## Make Your Own Nut and Seed Butter!

If you have a hand grain mill or electric blender, it's very easy to make fresh nut or seed butter. However, since cleaning a grain mill is rather a chore, it's a good idea to make several pounds of butter at a time.

It is always better to start out with unroasted nuts or seeds rather than buying already roasted ones. Roasting alters the quality of the oil, and the nuts and seeds go stale much more quickly, even when purchased from a reputable store.

Adjust your grain mill so that a fine paste is produced on the initial grinding, for the nut butter cannot be put through a mill twice. Add salt after grinding—about ½ teaspoon is plenty for each cup of nut butter.

Electric blenders should be set at "grind." It is important to grind only a small amount of nuts at a time, adding a little oil to make a paste consistency.

Butters will keep well without refrigeration if stored in clean airtight glass jars—provided they are not adulterated with water or flavoring agents.

If you accidently overroast the nuts or seeds, the oil becomes cooked and the butters will not be creamy. However, this mealy stuff is good in cookie, cake, or bread batters and can be used in place of part of the flour.

## Almond Butter
*(Makes about 1½ cups)*

1 pound fresh whole almonds
Several tablespoons oil (if you are using a blender)
½ teaspoon sea salt

Preheat oven to 350° F.

Spread almonds out on a cookie sheet. Insert sheet in oven, and roast for about 15–20 minutes, stirring occasionally so that almonds will be uniformly roasted.

For hand grinding: Adjust mill so that almonds will come out in a fine paste; the milling stone should not be set too tight, or the paste will not be able to come out through the grinding wheel. Mix salt in after roasting and grinding.

For blender butter: grind just a handful of nuts at a time, adding oil gradually so a smooth paste is made. Add salt and mix well.

## Cashew Butter

Follow directions as above, but reduce roasting time—cashews have more oil than almonds and roast more quickly.

## Walnut Butter

Roast walnuts as for cashews.

## Miscellaneous Nut Butters

Try using pecans or a combination of the above nuts. Hard nuts, such as Brazil nuts, are very difficult to grind into butters.

## Peanut Butter
*(Makes about 1 pound)*

1 pound fresh peanuts without shells
½ teaspoon sea salt
Oil if you are using a blender

Preheat oven to 350° F.

Spread nuts out on a cookie sheet. Insert sheet in oven and roast nuts for about 30 minutes, stirring occasionally to prevent burning.

Grind as for making Almond Butter (above).

## Sesame Butter
*(Makes about 1 pound)*

1 pound fresh unhulled sesame seeds (either brown or black)
½ teaspoon sea salt
Oil if you are using a blender

Wash sesame seeds in a fine strainer, using cold running water. Drain well and dry-roast in a cast-iron skillet over a medium flame. Stir constantly to prevent burning. When the seeds are tan in color and begin to pop, remove from heat. One test to tell if the seeds are ready is to rub a seed between the index finger and thumb—if it is easily crushed, then the seeds are ready to be ground.

Follow directions as for making Almond Butter (above).

## Sunflower Butter

Dry-roast seeds as for Sesame Butter (above) (washing is unnecessary), or roast in the oven on a cookie sheet. Follow directions for making Almond Butter (above).

## Nut Spreads

These spreads are delicious on crackers, bread, or muffins. They can also be used to stuff dates or apples.

Add finely grated orange or tangerine rind to nut butter, along with finely chopped dried fruit and/or chopped nuts. Or, try adding a dash of vanilla, lemon, or orange extract to the nut butter.

If spreads are too thick for easy spreading, thin with a little fruit juice.

# Chapter 14. *Beverages*

I didn't think this book would be complete without a chapter devoted to beverages that can be enjoyed both in hot and cold weather. These recipes are fun because they are so flexible and can be easily altered to suit your sweet tooth.

Included are recipes for making your own "organic" soft drinks, thick shakes (made without dairy products), and a few exotic recipes collected from friends who also love to experiment.

## *Almond Milk Shake*
*(Makes about 5 servings)*

1 cup almonds
Boiling water
4 cups fruit juice

Blanch the almonds by placing them in boiling water. Turn off the flame, cover pan, and let the nuts soak for 5–10 minutes, or until the skins slip off when squeezed between your fingers. Rinse the almonds in cold water and strain.

In a blender, liquefy the almonds with 1 cup fruit juice. Add remaining fruit juice and blend again. Chill before serving.

VARIATIONS: Oat Milk can be used in place of part of the fruit juice. Any combination of chopped dried fruit can be added in the blending process to sweeten the drink.

## Carob Almond Shake

Use 1 cup Carob Sauce and 1 cup water in place of 2 cups of the fruit juice. Pour into a freezer tray and chill until crystals begin to form around the edge of the tray.

## Coffee Almond Shake

Add 2 tablespoons dry grain coffee substitute (such as Pero) to Almond Milk Shake.

## Eggnog
(*Makes about 4 9-ounce servings*)

What would the holidays be like without this traditional favorite?

3 eggs, separated
2 tablespoons barley malt extract or Amasake Syrup
4 cups chilled Soy Milk
1 teaspoon vanilla extract
Nutmeg

Beat the egg whites until stiff; beat the yolks in a blender or by hand until foamy. Add barley malt to the yolks and beat again. Add soy milk and vanilla. Fold in egg whites. Flavor with nutmeg. Serve cold.

VARIATIONS: Mock Eggnog: Heat 4 cups soy milk with 2 tablespoons arrowroot flour starch or kuzu. Cook for a few minutes or until thick. Chill. Just before serving, beat in 2 tablespoons barley malt extract or amasake syrup and vanilla. Serve with a sprinkling of nutmeg.

## Fizzy Drinks

Naturally carbonated mineral water (found in liquor stores and health food stores) makes a pleasant mixer for refreshing soft drinks. Perrier or Vichy seems to have the best qualities for the following recipes.

## Apple Fizz
(*Makes 1 serving*)

Apple butter
Naturally carbonated mineral water
Slices of lemon

For each serving, place a large spoonful of apple butter in a tall glass. Add a small amount of mineral water and mix well. Tilt the glass slightly and pour in the desired amount of chilled mineral water. Serve with a thin slice of lemon.

## Carbonated Fruit Punch
(*Makes about 9 4-ounce servings*)

2 cups cherry cider
Orange and lemon slices
Juice of 2 oranges
1 pint carbonated mineral water

Combine cherry cider, fruit slices, and orange juice in a punch bowl. Cover and let sit in a refrigerator for several hours. Just before serving add mineral water. Pour over cups of cracked ice.

## Fizzy Lemonade
(*Makes about 5 servings*)

3 lemons
3 cups apple juice
Cracked ice
Large bottle of mineral water

Cut lemons in half and squeeze the juice into a saucepan. Grate about 1 tablespoon of lemon rind into the pan. Add apple juice and simmer for 10 minutes. Strain and cool until lukewarm. Pour over tall glasses filled with cracked ice and fill each glass to the top with mineral water.

VARIATIONS: Use limes or oranges in place of the lemons. Purple passion: Use grape juice instead of apple juice. If you prefer a sweeter drink, add a few tablespoons of Amasake Syrup to juice.

## Fresh Fruit Frappé
(*Makes 5–6 servings*)

2 cups fruit juice or Fruit Nectar
¼ cup Sesame Butter or Almond Butter (or any other)
1 pint fresh strawberries, blueberries, or crushed fruit
Ice

Combine fruit juice and nut butter in a blender. Add fresh fruit and blend again. Add ice until drink reaches desired consistency. Serve immediately.

VARIATIONS: Freeze the fresh fruit for several hours and blend as above instead of adding ice for a thicker drink.

Oat Milk can be used in place of some of the fruit juice.

## Fruit Nectar
*(Makes 6 large servings)*

5 pounds of fresh fruit (apricots, peaches, or pears, etc.)
1–2 cups water
Dash of salt

Wash, core, and quarter the fruit. Place in a heavy saucepan or pressure cooker. For pressure cooking, add 1 cup water and salt and cook under medium pressure for 20 minutes. If boiling, use 2 cups water; bring fruit to a boil with water, add salt, and cover. Simmer for 45 minutes. Strain fruit to obtain nectar. Use leftover fruit pulp for puddings or muffin batters.

## Fruit Concentrate
*(Makes about 3 cups)*

Simmer Fruit Nectar (above) in a heavy saucepan over a low flame until liquid is reduced to about ⅓ of its original volume. This concentrate can be used as a sweetening agent in place of maple syrup or honey. Keep refrigerated.

## Grain Coffee
*(Makes enough for 48 cups)*

There are several excellent varieties of instant and "percolator" grain coffees available in health and natural food stores. However, it is easy and inexpensive to grind a batch of your own if you have a grain mill or blender.

½ cup soybeans
1 cup rye berries
1 cup barley

Soak the soybeans in enough water to cover for 12 hours, changing the water halfway through soaking. Drain and rinse and spread on a cookie sheet. Spread rye berries and barley on a separate cookie sheet. Bake all ingredients in a slow 200° F. oven for about 2 hours, stirring occasionally. Remove sheets when all grains and beans are well browned, almost black in color.

Grind to a consistency of corn meal for *percolator* grain coffee. Use 1 heaping tablespoon grain coffee for each pint of water and simmer for 10–15 minutes. Store coffee in airtight glass containers.

VARIATIONS: One-half cup roasted dandelion root or ¼ cup chicory can be added for extra strength. For a sweeter brew, add a small amount of chopped dried fruit when brewing the coffee.

## Malted Carob Drink
(*Makes 3–4 servings*)

1 cup Oat Milk or water
⅓ cup lightly toasted sunflower seeds (or sesame seeds or nuts)
2 tablespoons chopped dates or raisins
1 cup Carob Sauce
Ice

Combine oat milk in a blender with the seeds. Set speed to liquefy. Add dried fruit and carob sauce. Add ice until desired consistency is reached.

## Frozen Carob Malted
(*Makes 3–4 servings*)

Use 2 cups Oat Milk and eliminate ice in above recipe. Pour carob drink into a freezer tray and freeze until crystals begin to form. Serve immediately.

## Mock Beer
(*Makes 8 servings*)

This is a wild drink invented by an Irish friend of mine in California. Its bittersweet taste is very similar to a strong European beer or malt but without the alcohol.

1 pint water
Flower of hops
1 small knob fresh gingerroot or 1 teaspoon powder
Chilled apple juice or Amasake Syrup
1 quart chilled mineral water

Bring water to a boil and add a large spoonful of hops. Simmer for a few minutes. Let stand overnight. The longer the hops steep, the stronger the brew.

Peel the gingerroot and finely grate. Squeeze out the juice and discard the pulp. For serving: start out with a few tablespoons of the hops tea and a drop or two of the ginger juice in a glass. Add apple juice or amasake syrup to sweeten to taste and fill remaining portion of glass with mineral water. Each person can vary the strength and sweetness of this concoction to suit individual taste.

## Muesli Punch
(*Makes 5–6 servings*)

*Muesli* is the Swiss name for a mixture of grain, nuts, and fruits. It has many versions, and the following recipe can be varied to suit your taste by adding different fruits or nuts.

1 cup apple cider
½ cup raisins or currants
½ cup chopped dried apricots
½ cup toasted slivered almonds
3 cups Oat Milk (given below)
Cinnamon or nutmeg

Simmer the first 4 ingredients together in a covered saucepan for 15 minutes. Combine in a blender with the oat milk and served chilled with a dash of cinnamon or nutmeg.

This drink is particularly enjoyable in the winter when served hot with a cinnamon stick.

## Oat Milk
(*Makes 3 cups milk*)

1 cup uncooked whole oat groats (not oat flakes)
5 cups water
1 vanilla bean

Wash the groats and pressure-cook with water and vanilla bean for 45 minutes. For regular cooking, bring oats and water to a boil, add vanilla bean, cover pan and simmer for at least 1 hour. Remove vanilla bean and strain. The residue grain may be used for making bread, muffin, or cookie batter.

VARIATION: Use fruit juice in place of water for a sweeter version.

## Soy Milk
(*Makes 1 quart*)

You can use this sweet beverage in place of water or fruit juice in cake, bread, and cookie batters, or enjoy it plain with a few cookies. It is very much like regular cow's milk, but lower in calories and fat.

4 cups water
1 cup soybean flour or powder
¼ teaspoon sea salt
2 tablespoons barley malt extract
1 teaspoon vanilla

In a saucepan or double boiler, beat water and soybean flour together with a whisk to eliminate lumps. Bring to a boil over a medium flame. Add salt, lower flame, and simmer for 20 minutes.

Strain through several layers of cheesecloth to remove pulp. (Pulp may be used in bread, cookie, or cake batter.) Let cool; beat in barley malt and vanilla.

Stays fresh in the refrigerator for 2–3 days.

VARIATIONS: For carob-flavored drink: Add 1 tablespoon carob powder to each 8 ounces soy milk. Additional flavoring agents, such as almond or orange extract or Pero (a grain coffee substitute), are also good to use.

## Winter Punch
(*Makes 8 servings*)

1 bag mu tea
2 cinnamon sticks
A few cloves
4 cups water
4 cups apple cider
Lemon and orange slices

In a large pot bring mu tea, spices, and water to a boil. Cover and simmer for 20 minutes. Remove tea bag, add remaining ingredients, and simmer for another 10 minutes. Serve piping hot in coffee mugs.

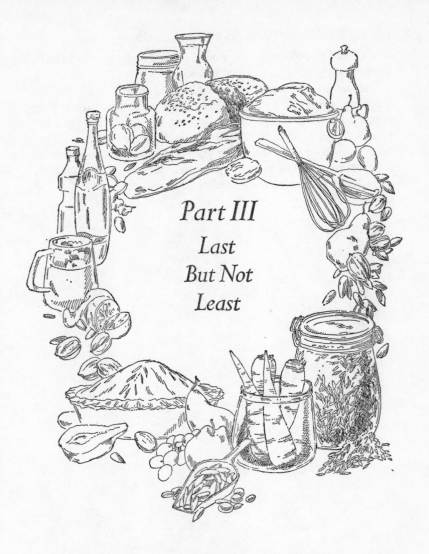

# Part III
## Last
## But Not
## Least

The food charts in the Appendix are designed as a quick reference guide for many of the foods used in this book, and therefore are not well detailed. For further information, there are a number of excellent books, such as "Composition of Foods," U. S. Agricultural Handbook No. 8 (it is available at public libraries, or it may be ordered from the U. S. Government Printing

Office) and *Composition and Facts About Foods,* by Ford Heritage (carried in natural and health food stores).

The guide to Natural and Health Food Stores is an aid for shopping across the country. Because so many new stores keep popping up while others become extinct, the guide will probably be a little out of date the day it is printed. However, it is hoped that it will come in handy, and if you should like to have a favorite store of yours listed that I've neglected to include, please write me a letter in care of the publisher so I can try to add it to the next edition.

# An Appendix of Food Value Charts

## Good Sources of Minerals
*(Foods Commonly Used in This Book)*

| Mineral | Recommended Daily Allowance Adult | Child | Food Source (in milligrams) | | Use in Body |
|---------|---------|-------|-------------|------|-------------|
| Calcium | .8 grams | 1.0–1.4 grams | Sesame seeds<br>Agar-agar<br>Almonds<br>Soybeans<br>Sunflower seeds | 1160<br>567<br>234<br>226<br>120 | Builds bones, teeth, muscle contraction, activates some enzymes, normalizes metabolism |
| Phosphorous | 1.2 grams | 2.0 grams | Wheat germ<br>Sunflower seeds<br>Almonds<br>Dried apricot | 1118<br>837<br>504<br>108 | Builds bones, teeth, blood, hair; activates some enzymes; nervous tissue, metabolism of fat |
| Potassium | 3.0 grams | 1.5 grams | Soybeans<br>Wheat bran<br>Dried apricot<br>Sunflower seeds | 1677<br>1121<br>979<br>920 | Regulates heartbeat; aids in elimination; aids in formation of glycogen from glucose, proteins from peptones and proteoses |
| Sodium | .5 grams | | Sesame seeds<br>Carrots<br>Sunflower seeds<br>Raisins | 60<br>47<br>30<br>27 | Aids in formation of digestive juices, elimination of carbon dioxide, maintains water balance |

| Mineral | Recommended Daily Allowance Adult | Child | Food Source (in milligrams) | | Use in Body |
|---|---|---|---|---|---|
| Magne-sium | 300 milligrams | | Wheat germ Soybeans Almonds Sesame seeds Millet Peanuts | 336 265 270 181 162 206 | Strengthens nerves and muscles; conditions liver and glands; stimulates elimination; activates enzymes in carbohydrate metabolism |
| Iron | 10–12 milligrams | 7–15 milligrams | Wheat bran Sesame seeds Agar-agar Prunes | 14.9 10.5 6.3 3.9 | Hemoglobin; oxidative enzymes, bones, brain muscle |
| Iodine | 0.15–0.30 milligrams | | Agar-agar Water-melon Blue-berry Straw-berry | .166 .040 .020 .019 | Aids in oxidation of fats, proteins; stimulates circulation |

Food values based on 3½ ounces of edible portion.

Data taken from *Composition and Facts About Foods* by Ford Heritage, Woodstown, New Jersey, 1968. Note: Heritage is both author and publisher.

## Nutritional Value of Foods Used Frequently in This Book

| Fruit | I.U.* Vitamin A | In mg† Vitamin C | Calories | (Values in Grams) Carbohydrates | Fats | Protein |
|---|---|---|---|---|---|---|
| Apple | 90 | 7 | 56 | 14.1 | .6 | .2 |
| Apricot, fresh | 2700 | 10 | 51 | 12.8 | .2 | 1.0 |
| dried | 10,900 | 12 | 260 | 66.5 | .5 | 5.0 |
| Blueberry | 100 | 14 | 62 | 15.3 | .5 | 1.2 |

| Fruit | I.U.* Vitamin A | In mg† Vitamin C | Calories | (Values in Grams) Carbohydrates | Fats | Protein |
|---|---|---|---|---|---|---|
| Cherry, sweet | 110 | 10 | 70 | 17.4 | .4 | .3 |
| Currant | 230 | 200 | 54 | 13.1 | .1 | 1.7 |
| Date | 50 | 0 | 274 | 72.9 | .5 | 2.2 |
| Fig, dried | 80 | 2 | 274 | 69.1 | 1.3 | 4.3 |
| Lemon, whole | 30 | 77 | 27 | 8.2 | .3 | 1.1 |
| Orange | 250 | 110 | 40 | 15.5 | .2 | 1.3 |
| Peach | 1330 | 7 | 38 | 9.7 | .1 | .6 |
| Pear | 20 | 4 | 61 | 15.3 | .4 | .7 |
| Prune | 1600 | 3 | 255 | 67.4 | .6 | 2.1 |
| Raisin | 20 | 1 | 289 | 77.4 | .2 | 2.5 |
| Strawberry | 60 | 59 | 37 | 8.4 | .5 | .7 |
| Watermelon | 590 | 7 | 26 | 6.4 | .2 | .5 |
| *Vegetable* | | | | | | |
| Carrot | 11,000 | 8 | 42 | 9.7 | .2 | 1.1 |
| Parsnip | 30 | 16 | 76 | 17.5 | .5 | 1.7 |
| Pumpkin | 1600 | 9 | 26 | 6.5 | .1 | 1.0 |
| Squash | 3700 | 32 | 50 | 12.4 | .3 | 1.4 |

\* International units.   † Milligrams.

Food values based upon 3½ ounces of edible portion. Data taken from *Composition and Facts About Foods,* by Ford Heritage.

## Food values based upon 3½ ounces of edible portion.

| FOOD | Calories | Carbohydrates in grams | Fats in grams | Protein in grams |
|---|---|---|---|---|
| *Seeds* | | | | |
| Sesame | 563 | 21.6 | 49.1 | 18.6 |
| Sunflower | 560 | 19.9 | 47.3 | 24.0 |
| *Nuts* | | | | |
| Almonds | 598 | 19.5 | 54.2 | 18.6 |
| Cashews | 561 | 29.3 | 47.5 | 17.2 |
| Chestnuts | | | | |
| (fresh) | 194 | 42.1 | 1.5 | 2.9 |
| Walnuts | 628 | 14.8 | 59.3 | 20.5 |
| *Beans* | | | | |
| Peanuts | 564 | 18.6 | 47.5 | 26.0 |
| Soybeans | | | | |
| (dried) | 403 | 33.5 | 17.7 | 34.1 |

| FOOD | Calories | Carbohydrates in grams | Fats in grams | Protein in grams |
|---|---|---|---|---|
| *Grains* | | | | |
| Barley | 348 | 77.6 | 1.1 | 9.6 |
| Buckwheat (flour) | 347 | 72.0 | 2.5 | 11.7 |
| Corn | 355 | 73.7 | 3.9 | 9.2 |
| Millet | 327 | 72.9 | 2.9 | 9.9 |
| Oats | 390 | 68.2 | 7.4 | 14.2 |
| Rice (brown) | 360 | 77.4 | 1.9 | 7.5 |
| Rice bran | 276 | 50.8 | 15.8 | 13.3 |
| Rye | 334 | 73.4 | 1.7 | 12.1 |
| Wheat, hard spring | 330 | 69.1 | 2.2 | 14.0 |
| Wheat bran | 213 | 61.9 | 4.6 | 16.0 |
| Wheat germ | 363 | 46.7 | 10.9 | 26.6 |

Data from "Composition of Foods," U. S. Agricultural Handbook No. 8, and *Composition and Facts About Foods,* by Ford Heritage.

# Guide to Natural and Health Food Stores

*Alaska*

Super Natural Foods
3906 Greenland Drive
Anchorage 99501

*Arizona*

Natural Health Foods
4225 E. Camelbade Rd.
Phoenix 85001

Vitality Health Foods, Inc.
18 S. Central Ave.
Phoenix 85001

Food for Thought
1922 E. Hendrick St.
Tucson 85702

The Granary
1955 E. Hendrick St.
Tucson 85702

*Arkansas*

Old Fashioned Food, Inc.
123 N. 18th St.
Fort Smith 72901

Shiloh Farms
Rte. 59
Sulfur Springs 72768

*California*

Whole Earth Natural Foods
935 G St.
Arcata 95521

The Mustard Seed
Town and Country Shopping Center

Mill Valley and Telegraph Ave.
Berkeley 94704

Wholly Foods
2999 Shattuck Ave.
Berkeley 94709

The General Store
5th St. between Mission and
    Junipero
Carmel 93924

The Family Store
Bernadelli Square
Carmel Valley 93924

Chico San Foods
1144 West First St.
Chico 95926

Etidorpha Natural Foods
114 W. Twelfth St.
Chico 95926

Spiral Foods
1017 Willow St.
Chico 95926

The Granary
1220 La Plaza
Cotati 92428

Natural Gas Works
1063 Olive Drive
Davis 95616

Escondido Health Foods
405 W. Grand Ave.
Escondido 92025

The Good Earth
123 Bolinas Rd.
Fairfax 94930

Sun and Earth Natural Foods
6576 Trigo Rd.
Goleta 93017

Tao Natural Foods
371 Redondo Ave.
Long Beach 90801

Erewhon Trading Co. of L.A.
8003 Beverly Blvd.
Los Angeles 90048

Good Morning Natural Foods
242 Commercial St.
Nevada City 95959

Sacramento Real Food Co.
1500 Q St.
Sacramento 95800

Everybody's Natural Foods
1 Saunders Ave.
San Anselmo 94960

Clement Street Natural Foods
522 Clement St.
San Francisco 94118

Far Fetched Foods
1915 Page St.
San Francisco 94117

Hirschfelder Co.
1050 Howard St.
San Francisco 94102

Hunza Natural Foods
728 Vallejo St.
San Francisco 94100

Sonoma Natural Foods
3214 Folsom St.
San Francisco 94110

Harmony Food Co.
P.O. Box 1131
Santa Cruz 95060

Pacific Grain & Grocery
817 Pacific Ave.
Santa Cruz 95060

Rock Island Line Organic Food
Trip
1915 A Bridgeway
Sausalito 94965

Sonoma Natural Foods
4411 Gravenstein Highway North
Sebastopol 95965

*Colorado*

Art of Living Co-op
519 Concord Ave.
Boulder 80302

Green Mountain Granary
1804 Fourteenth St.
Boulder 80301

Ceres Harvest Natural Foods
2527 W. Colorado Ave.
Colorado Springs 80904

Charles Health Foods
P.O. Box 117
Creste Butte 81224

Living Foods Store
2634 W. Twenty-third Ave.
Denver 80211

*Connecticut*

Prospect Mt. Farm
Bantam 06790

Helbing's Delicatessen
Railroad St.
Canaan 06018

Healthwell Natural Food Shop
356 Greenwich Ave.
Greenwich 06830

Horn of Plenty
486 Thames St.
Groton 06340

The Alternative
2614 Boston Post Rd.
Guildford 06437

Cambridge Coffee Tea and Spice
House
93 Pratt St.
Hartford 06101

Good Food Store
295 Washington St.
Hartford 06101

Nature's Harvest
47 Chamberlin Highway
Kesington 06037

Wayne's Health Food Center
Middletown Shopping Center
Middletown 06457

Natural Foods
20 Forrest St.
New Caanan 06840

Fatone Brothers
625 Bank St.
New London 06320

The Fifth Season
165 Bank St.
New London 06320

Healthway Diet Center
60 Broadway
Norwich 06360

White Hart Inn
New England Country Store
Salisbury 06068

Not by Bread Alone
Farrell Rd.
Storrs 06268

The Health Food Loft
Box 261, Rte. 83
Talcotville 06066

Evergreen Good Food Co.
499 Danbury Rd.
Wilton 06897

*District of Columbia*

Gazang
3056 M St. N.W.
Washington 20007

Glut Washington Food
2323½ Eighteenth St. N.W.
Washington 20009

Yes
1039 Thirty-first St. N.W.
Washington 20007

*Florida*

Oak Feed Store
2825 Oak Ave., ₦15
Coconut Grove 33133

Scarborough's Health Food Stores
1441 N. Dixie Highway
Fort Lauderdale 33304

Scarborough's Health Food Stores
623 S. Sixtieth Ave.

K Mart Shopping Center
Hollywood 33022

The Come Together Natural Food
Shopper
426 N.E. Sixty-fifth St.
Miami 33101

Hale's Health Foods
Northside Shopping Center
Miami 33147

Healthful Diet Shoppe
1374 N.E. 163rd St.
North Miami Beach 33162

Feedbag General Store
Route 159, Rte. 4
Pensacola 32504

Perrine Health Foods, Inc.
770 Perrine Blvd.
Perrine 33314

Scarborough's Health Food Stores
4028 Bryan Blvd.
Plantation 33314

Tree of Life
c/o J & L Stores, Inc.
200 Anastasia Blvd.
St. Augustine 32089

Tree of Life
120 Sixth St. S.
St. Petersburg 33733

Sarasota Food Co-op
1551 Main St.
Sarasota 33578

Second Story Shop
109½ E. College Ave.
Tallahassee 32302

*Georgia*

Aquarian Health Food
3340 Peach Tree Rd.
Atlanta 30308

Atlanta Nutrition Center
571 Peach Tree N.E.
Atlanta 30308

Morning Star
1451–53 Oxford Rd.
Atlanta 30301

The Egg & the Lotus
1782 Cheshire Bridge Rd.
Atlanta 30301

The Good Earth
375 Pharr Rd. N.E.
Atlanta 30305

Ad Infinitum
130 College
Athens 30601

*Hawaii*

Fourth World General Store
72 Kapiolani St.
Hilo 96720

Good Earth
3520 Waialae Ave.
Honolulu 96813

*Illinois*

Fruitful Yield
6606 W. Cermack
Berwyn 60402

Mr. Natural Food Store
102 E. Jackson St.
Carbondale 62901

Earth & Sea Natural Organic Foods
2437 W. Eleventh St.
Chicago 60655

Food for Life
2478 N. Lincoln Ave.
Chicago, 60614

House of Gandhi
1457 E. Fifty-third St.
Chicago 60654

Hyde Park Health Foods
1360 E. Fifty-third St.
Chicago 60615

The Growth and Life Store
2937 N. Clark St.
Chicago 60657

The Health Food Shoppe
642½ W. Diversey
Chicago 60657

The Sandpiper
1511 W. Howard St.
Chicago 60625

Kishwaukee Valley Grainery
505 E. Lincoln Highway
De Kalb 60115

Here's Health Food
11 Douglas Ave.
Elgin 60120

Aquarian Dawn
314 E. Vandalia St.
Edwardsville, 62025

Diet House
1029 Davis St.
Evanston 60201

Green Earth
1914 Central Ave.
Evanston 60201

Diet House North
1826 N. Second St.
Highland Park 60035

Sunrise Farm Store
17650 Torrence Ave.
Lansing 60438

Whole Earth & Grain Depot
1162 Westgate
Oak Park 60302

Health House of Park Ridge
36 Main St.
Park Ridge 60068

Earth Foods—Earthworks
1310 Main St.
Urbana 61801

Moss Hill Organic Food & Provision Co.
6155 S. Cass Ave.
Westmont 60559

*Indiana*

The Clear Moment
116 N. Grant
Bloomington 47401

Open Market
312 W. Fourteenth St.
Bloomington 47401

Gerber's Nutrition
111 N. Main St.
Bluffton 47614

The Good Earth Natural Food Co.
6350 Guilford Ave.
Indianapolis 46206

Grainery
100 Center
Mishawaka

Witherspoon's Natural Foods
335 Northwestern Ave.
West Lafayette, 47906

*Iowa*

Maple St. Natural Foods
400 S. Central Ave.
Burlington 52601

The Food Trip
2018 College St.
Cedar Falls 50613

The Folks & Uncle Leonard
220 Fourth St. Tracks
Cedar Rapids 52401

Hybrid's Natural Foods
924 S. Sixth St.
Council Bluffs 51501

Federal Health Foods
Minna Vollum
308 Main St.
Davenport 52802

Good Earth Foods
1518 Harrison St.
Davenport 52800

Earth Natural Foods
3013 University Ave.
Des Moines 50311

Van's Health Foods
Rte. 2
Grinnell 50112

New Pioneer's Co-op Society
518 Bowery St.
Iowa City 52240

Mt. Vernon General
c/o Pat Young
103 First St. W.
Mt. Vernon 52314

*Kentucky*

The Grainery 137
1375 Bardstown Rd.
Louisville 40204

Revival
854 E. High St.
Lexington 40502

*Louisiana*

Vitality Food Shoppe
4213 Government St.
Baton Rouge 70806

Fine Foods
3236 S. Carrollten Ave.
New Orleans 70118

Shambala
1201 Decatur St.
New Orleans 70116

Something Beautiful
717 Dante St.
New Orleans 70118

*Maine*

Seven Seas
West Gate Mall
Bangor 04401

Hunt's Health Foods
56 Weymouth St.
Brunswick 04011

Feeding   Acres   Natural   Organic
   Food
Gorham 04038

Port Food Co-op
Dock Square
Kennebunkport 04046

Axis Natural Foods, Inc.
255 Lisbon St.
Lewiston 04240

Donn's Health Foods
14 Oak St.
Lisbon Falls 04252

Good Day Market
370 Fore St.
Portland 04101

Model Food
113–115 Middle St.
Portland 04111

Root Cellar
246 Main St.
P.O. Box 574
Rockland 04841

Natural Foods
105 Water St.
Waterville 04901

Health Food Store
Middle St. S.
Wiscasset 04578

*Maryland*

Sun & Earth
1923 Third St.
Annapolis 21403

Diet & Health Foods
Reisterstown Rd. Plaza
Baltimore 21233

Good Earth Organic Grocery
823 Charles St.
Baltimore 21231

Beautiful Day Trading Co.
4915 Berwyn Rd.
College Park 20740

Spring Bottom Natural Foods
53 Bottom Rd.
Hydes 21082

Sundance Brotherhood
9 N. Division St.
Ocean City 21842

Kennedy's Natural Foods Inc.
Baltimore Rd. and Rte. 28
Rockville 20851

*Massachusetts*

Kim Toy Foods
32 Amity St.
Amherst 01002

Laughing Gravey
1 Cook Pl.
Amherst 01002

Whole Wheat Trading Co.
181 N. Pleasant
Amherst 01002

Stern's National Food Center
261 Cabot Rd.
Beverly 01915

Erewhon Trading Co.
342 Newbury St.
Boston 02109

Good Food Store
814 Beacon St.
Boston 02109

Life Foods
1349 Commonwealth Ave.
Brighton 02135

Attar
31 Putnam Ave.
Cambridge 02139

Corners of the Mouth Restaurant
   & Store
1419 Cambridge St.
Cambridge 02140

Walden Organic Market
272 Walden St.
Cambridge 02138

Chatham Natural Food Market
587 Main St.
Chatham 02633

Life Naturganic Food Market
480 Main St.
Chatham 02633

American Health Foods
213 W. Plain St.
Cochituate 01778

Concord Spice & Grain
191 Sudbury Rd.
Concord 01742

Yellow Sun Natural Foods Co-op
P.O. Box 104
Conway 01341

Wendway Natural Foods
P.O. Box 12
Edgartown 02539

Mother Earth
25 Queens Byway
Falmouth 02540

Pure & Simple
37 Elm St.
Fitchburg 01420

Blossom St. Market
143 Blossom St.
Fitchburg 01420

The Life Preserver
280 Worcester Rd.
Framingham 01701

The Natural Food Store
Simon's Rock
Great Barrington 02130

Russell's County Store
94 Central St.
Holliston 01746

Natural Answer
P.O. Box 822
481 Pleasant St.
Holyoke 01040

Nature's Pantry
Main St.
Lakeville Plaza
Lakeville 02346

The Source
50 Central St.
Leominster 01453

Alchemist
96 Main St.
Maynard 01754

House of Natural Foods
100 Main St.
Milford 07157

Natural Food Market
1668 Acushnet Ave.
New Bedford 02740

Natural Health Foods
822 E. Washington St.
North Attleboro 02760

The Granary
48 Old S. St.
Northhampton 01060

Cape Cod Health Food center
16 Westbay Rd.
Osterville 02655

Natural Foods
47 North St.
Pittsfield 01201

Earth Foods
214 Commercial St.
Provincetown 02657

Healthway Food Shop
235 Elm St.
Somerville 02143

The Health Hut
14 Elm St.
Southbridge 01550

Life New Health Foods
1274 Washington St.
West Newton 02181

Organic Foods
557 Bedford St.
Whitman 02382

Health and Diet
386 W. J. Boyleston St.
Worcester 01601

Living Earth
327 Pleasant St.
Worcester 01601

*Michigan*

Eden Organic Food Store
211 S. State St.
Ann Arbor 48108

Vim & Vigor, Inc.
210 S. Woodward St.
Continental Market
Birmingham 48011

Joyous Revival
1801 S. Woodward
Birmingham 48011

Health Unlimited
5255 Schaefer St.
Dearborn 48124

Open City Food Co-op
4551 Third St.
Detroit 48201

Rocky Peanut Co.
2453 Russell St.
Detroit 48207

Family of Man, Inc.
201½ E. Grand River St.
East Lansing 48823

Sauer's Vita Health Foods
16463 Woodward St.
Highland Park 48203

Sun Traditional Foods
141 Burr Oak St.
Kalamazoo 49001

Serbo's Foods
34164 Plymouth Rd.
Livonia 48150

The Carrot Patch
6672 Orchard Lake Rd.
Orchard Lake 48033

Nutri Foods, Inc.
120 S. Main St.
Royal Oak 48067

*Minnesota*

Carol Natural Foods
811 La Salle
Minneapolis 55414

Shaktih Organic Foods
604 W. Twenty-sixth St.
Minneapolis 55408

Tao Traditional Foods
3449 Cedar Ave.
Minneapolis 55407

*Mississippi*

The Granary
3003 N. State St.
Jackson 39206

Zap Boutique
4911 N. State St.
Jackson 39206

*Missouri*

Chrysalis
8860 Ladue Rd.
St. Louis 63124

Morning Dew
6002 Pershing St.
St. Louis 63166

New Dawn Natural Foods, Inc.
3175 S. Grand Blvd.
St. Louis 63118

*Nevada*

Buddy's Health Foods
953 E. Sahara Ave.
Las Vegas 89105

*New Hampshire*

New England People's Co-op
Rte. 123A
Alstead 03602

Galef's Country Store, Inc.
Barrington 03825

Granite State Natural Foods
494 N. State St.
Concord 03301

Mattapoisett House
P.O. Box 136, Main St.
Dublin 03048

Brookwood Ecology Center
Box 51, Rte. 1
Greenville 03048

Erewhon Farms Store
195 Winchester St.
Keene 03431

Natural Foods
752 Main St.
Laconia 03246

The Source
40 Main St.
Lancaster 03584

Honey Gardens
227 Mechanic St.
Lebanon 03766

Earth Things
70 Market St.
Manchester 03105

Nutrition House
1269 Elm St.
Manchester 03101

The Old Country Store
Moultonboro 03254

Center of Aquarius Health Foods
295 Daniel Webster Highway
Nashua 03060

Port O' Call
137 Main St.
Nashua 03060

Living Earth Farm
Rte. 5
Penacock 03301

The Village Store
South Acworth City 03607

Kellerhaus
P.O. Box 356, Rte. 3
Weirs Beach 03246

Do It
52 Main St.
West Lebanon 03784

*New Jersey*

Natro Health Foods
268 Morris Ave.
Elizabeth 07207

Food for Thought
15 Park Ave.
Madison 07940

Montclair Health Foods
549 Bloomfield Ave.
Montclair 07042

The Health Shoppe
151 Morris St.
Morristown 07960

Back to the Garden Health Food
Store
43 Paterson St.
New Brunswick 08901

Whole Earth Center of Princeton
173 Nassau St.
Princeton 08540

Third Day
10 Franklin Pl.
Rutherford 07070

Good Life Health Food Shoppe
Barnstable Court
Saddle River 07458

The Health Food Shoppe
299 Bellevue Ave.
Upper Montclair 07043

*New Mexico*

The Good Earth Natural Food
Store
P.O. Box 117
Arroyo Seco 97514

Natural Foods
1203 Cerrillos Rd.
Sante Fe 87501

Hummingbird Shop
P.O. Box 1151
Taos 87571

*New York*

Earth Foods
238 Washington Ave.
Albany 12201

The Store
277 Lark
Albany 12201

Off Center
The Off Campus College's Commu-
nity Store
73 State St.
Binghamton 13902

Nature's Nest
1726 Jerome Ave.
Brooklyn 11235

Allentown Food Co-op
180 N. Pearl St.
Buffalo 14240

The Main St. Grainary #1
15 Main St.
Chatham 12037

Potlatch
5 Tompkins St.
Cortland 13045

Hidlegaard's
University Plaza
Eggertsville 14217

Sunrise Health Food Store
148 Canal St.
Ellenville 12428

Tsujimoto
6530 Seneca St.
Elma 14059

Queens Organic Foods
156–05 Forty-fifth Ave.
Flushing 11355

Farm Store
Rte. 1
Fly Creek 13337

Natural Foods Farm Store
Rte. 1
Fly Creek 13337

Pullman Diet Foods, Inc.
21 N. Franklin St.
Hempstead 11550

Sun Natural Food
7 South Seventh St.
Hudson 12534

Korrect Health Foods
Korvette Shopping Center
370-B, Rte. 110
Huntington Station 11746

Ithaca Food Conspiracy
107 S. Aurora St.
Ithaca 14850

Ithaca Seed Co.
107½ Dryden St.
Ithaca 14850

Belly of the Whale
271 Floral Ave.
Johnson City 13790

Colonial Health Foods Center, Inc.
43 Front St.
Kingston 12401

The Store
Main St.
Margarettville 12455

Movement
350 Broadway
Monticello 12701

Real Food Store
53 Main St.
New Paltz 12561

Caldron's Well
308 E. Sixth St.
New York 10003

Good Earth
1336 First Ave.
New York 10021

Greenberg's
125 First Ave.
New York 10003

Mother Nature & Sons
351 Bleecker St.
New York 10014

Mr. Natural Comes to the City
191 E. Third St.
New York 10009

Nature's Cupboard
80 E. Seventh St.
New York 10003

Panacea
323 Third Ave.
New York 10010

Shaping Grain
49 W. Seventy-second St., 9b
New York 10023

Tuvya
325 E. Fifty-fourth St.
New York 10022

Whole Earth Provisions
156 First Ave.
New York 10009

L & L Health Food Store
Shookville Rd.
Red Hook 12571

Dietary Specialties
1 Cottage St.
Rochester 14608

The Health Food Company
649 Monroe Ave.
Rochester 14603

C. T. Yang
1673 Mount Hope
Rochester 16620

Staff of Life Natural Foods
502 N. James St.
Rome 13440

Never When Inc.
18 Main St.
Roslyn 11576

Saratoga Traders
16 Caroline St.
Saratoga Springs 12866

Mother Nature's Nutrition
76 Garth Rd.
Scarsdale 10583

Eco-Symbio Co-op
249 Dunnsville Rd.
Schenectady 12306

The Natural Way
78 Sabonac Rd.
Southampton 11968

State University of N.Y.
Stonybrook Health Food Co-op
Rm. 044 Student Union Bldg.
Stonybrook 11790

Juniper Farms
Box 100
Sugar Loaf 10981

Brad's Brews, Victuals & Stews
713 S. Crouse Ave.
Syracuse 13210

Central Purchasing Co-op
459 Westcott St.
Syracuse 13201

Nature's Pantry
122 Trinity Place
Syracuse 13210

Troy Nutritious Foods
451 Fulton St.
Troy 12180

Good Seed
Walkill Ave.
Walkill 12589

Sunflower
107 Tinker St.
Woodstock 12498

Woodstock's Health Foods
10 Mill Hill Rd.
Woodstock 12498

*North Carolina*

The Green Revolution
(N & N Associates)
106 Howard St.
Boone 28607

Harmony
112 Lloyd St.
Carrboro 27515

Earth Inc.
412 Franklin St.
Chapel Hill 27514

Sunrise Health Foods
510 Cotanche St.
Greenville 27834

*North Dakota*

Tochi Products
303 Roberts St.
Fargo 58102

Something of Value
618 Third St., N.E.
Minot 58701

*Ohio*

Alexander's Health Foods
282 S. Main St.
Akron 44308

Firelands Country Store
Rte. 113
Amherst 44001

The Farmacy
13 West State St.
Athens 45701

Food for Thought
118 W. Woorster St.
Bowling Green 43402

Eden Natural Foods
347 Ludlow Ave.
Cincinnati 45220

Reality Foods
1126 Carney St.
Cincinnati 45202

Wholesome Earth
2615 Vine St.
Cincinnati 45219

Genesis 1–29
12200 Euclid Ave.
Cleveland 44101

Vitality Health Food Shop, Inc.
51 The Old Arcade
Cleveland 44101

The Food Project
2800 Mayfield Rd., No. 208
Cleveland Heights 44118

Morning Star Organic Foods
1714 N. High St.
Columbus 43201

Kent Natural Foods
135 S. Water St.
Kent 44240

Pluggy's Town Store
P.O. Box 501–2 E. Winter
Delaware 43015

Good Foods Co-op
Co-op Bookstore
37 College St. W.
Oberlin 44074

Adam Sigerson
Box 157, Rte. 1
Rutland 45775

Real Good Food Co-op
Antioch College
Yellow Springs 45387

*Oklahoma*

L & L Health Foods Company
Box 197, Rte. 1
Fairview 73737

Nutritional Food Center
1024 Classen Blvd.
Oklahoma City 73125

Roger Randolph
1228 E. Twenty-ninth Pl.
Tulsa 74114

*Oregon*

Friends of the Earth
41 Third St.
Ashaland 97520

Merrick's Natural Foods
200 N.W. D. St.
Grants Pass 97526

*Pennsylvania*

Pennyfeather
Rtes. 2 & 100
Chadds Ford 19317

Natural Health Foods
422 Main St.
Edwardsville 18704

Essene
320 South St.
Philadelphia 19147

Zeitlyn
1025 Westview St.
Philadelphia 19101

Good Earth Natural Foods
2218 Murray Ave.
Pittsburgh 15230

Health House, Inc.
1414 Potomac Ave.
Pittsburgh 15216

John McKee Bell's Natural Foods
5402 Walnut St.
Pittsburgh 15232

New Life Natural Foods Co.
1138 Northway Mall
McKnight Rd.
Pittsburgh 15230

*Rhode Island*

Alternative Co-op
78 Biscuit City Rd.
Kingston 02881

The Good Earth
24 Memorial Blvd.
Newport 02840

Cass Ave. Health Center
1025 Cass Ave.
Woonsocket 02895

*South Carolina*

Sunshine Health Foods
14 B. St. Phillips St.
Charleston 29401

*South Dakota*

Harvest Moon Foods
9 W. National St.
Vermillion 57069

*Tennessee*

Whole Foods General Store
1783 Union Ave., Rear
Memphis 38104

New Morning
1004 Sixteenth Ave. S.
Nashville, 37212

*Texas*

Natural Foods and Country Store
1911 Ayers St.
Corpus Christi 78404

Realife Health, Inc.
4441 Lovers Lane
Dallas 75225

Arrowhead Mills
P.O. Box 866
Hereford 79045

A Movable Feast
908 Westheimer
Houston 77008

Staff of Life
2037 West Alabama St.
Houston 77008

Tao Whole Foods
15 Waugh Drive
Houston 77007

*Utah*

Goddard's Health Food Mart
3427 Riverdale Rd.
Ogden 84403

Scheibner's Health Center
280 West First N.
Provo 84601

Scheibner's Health Center
158 S. State St.
Salt Lake City 84111

Gwaltney's Natural Foods
Cottonwood Mall
Salt Lake City 84121

*Vermont*

Gingerbread Natural Foods
201 Depot St.
Bennington 05201

Spice n' Nice
c/o Country Farm Store
209 N. Bennington Rd.
Bennington 05201

The Good Life
P.O. Box 282
Brattleboro 05301

Guilford Country Store
Rte. 3
Brattleboro 05301

Natural Universe
103 Main St.
Brattleboro 05301

Solanaceae Natural Foods
115 N. Winooski St.
Burlington 05401

Healy, Inc.
Manchester Depot 05256

Om Natural Health Foods
15 Court St.
Middlebury 05753

Store Two
2 Park St.
Middlebury 05753

Wholemeal
30 College St.
Poultney 05764

Bungaree Natural Foods
RFD 1, Rte. 5
Putney 05346

Bulter's Pantry
RFD 1
Putney 05346

Zodiac Health Foods
Rte. 5
Putney 05346

Ripton Country Store, Inc.
Box 60, Rte. 125
Ripton 05766

Cold River Farm
21 Center St.
Rutland 05701

Hatch Memorial Library & Store
8 Pine St.
St. Johnsbury 05819

Sunshine Natural Products
63 Eastern Ave.
St. Johnsbury 05819

Old Mill Store
Rte. 106
South Woodstock 05071

Tweedmeadown Natural Foods
Stockbridge 05772

Warren Store
Warren 05674

Tamarack Farm Mill & Bakery
Weston 05161

Natural Foods, Wee Ski Shop
Main St.
Wilmington 05363

Yankee Clipper
3 E. Eallen St.
Winooski 05404

*Virginia*

Kennedy's Natural Foods, Inc.
1500 Wilson Blvd.
Arlington 22209

Kennedy's Natural Foods, Inc.
1051 W. Broad St.
Falls Church 22046

Kennedy's Natural Foods, Inc.
6801 Springfield Plaza
Springfield 22150

Store
110 Washington St.
Lexington 24450

*Washington*

Capitol Hill Co-op
Twelfth and Denny
Seattle 98122

Erewhon Trading Co.
3424 N.E. Fifty-fifth St.
Seattle 98105

*Wisconsin*

Good Earth General
919 East Main St.
Green Bay 54301

Good Earth Foods, Ltd.
1315 Redfield
La Crosse 54601

Concordance Natural Foods
301 S. State St.
Madison 53703

Whole Earth Co-op
817 E. Johnson St.
Madison 53703

Outpost—ICC
800 E. Clark
Milwaukee 53212

Good Life Natural Foods
600 N. Main St.
Oshkosh 54901

# *Wholesale Distributors in the United States*

*Arkansas*

Shiloh Farms
Rte. 59
Sulfur Springs 72768

*California*

Erewhon Trading Co. of L.A.
8003 W. Beverly Blvd.
Los Angeles 90048

Chico San Foods
1144 West First St.
Chico 95926

*Illinois*

Food for Life
420 Wrightwood
Elmhurst 60126

*Massachusetts*

Erewhon Trading Co.
33 Farnsworth St.
Boston 02210

*New York*

Deer Valley Farms
Guilford 13780

Infinity Food Co.
171 Duane
New York 10013

Juniper Farms
Box 100
Sugar Loaf 10981

*North Dakota*

Pioneer Specialty Foods
Fargo 58100

*Pennsylvania*

Merit Food Company
Pill Hill Lane
Box 177
Bally 19503

*Natural Herbs only:*

Celestial Seasonings
Box 1405
1027 Pine St.
Boulder, Colorado 80302

Meadowbrook Herb Garden
Rte. 138
Wyoming, Rhode Island 02898

# Bibliography

Abrahamson, Emanuel Maurice, M.D., and Pezet, A. W., *Body, Mind and Sugar*, New York, Henry Holt and Company, 1948.

"Composition of Food," U. S. Agricultural Handbook No. 8.

Davis, Adelle, *Let's Cook It Right*, New York, New American Library, 1971.

Goldstein, J., and Goldman, M. C., eds., *Guide to Organic Food Shopping and Organic Living*, Emmaus, Pa., Rodale Books, 1971.

Heritage, Ford, *Composition and Facts About Foods*, Woodstown, N.J., Ford Heritage, 1968.

Jacob, H. E., *Six Thousand Years of Bread*, Garden City, New York, Doubleday and Company, 1945.

Longgood, William, *The Poisons in Your Food*, New York, Grove Press, 1970.

McCane, Robert Alexander, and Widdowson, Elsie May, *The Chemical Composition of Foods*, New York, Chemical Publishing Co., 1940.

Nicholls, John Ralph, *Aids to Analysis of Food and Drugs*, London, Balliere, Tindall and Cox, 1952.

Yudkin, Dr. John, *Sweet and Dangerous*, New York, Peter H. Wyden, Inc., 1972.

# INDEX